I0605602

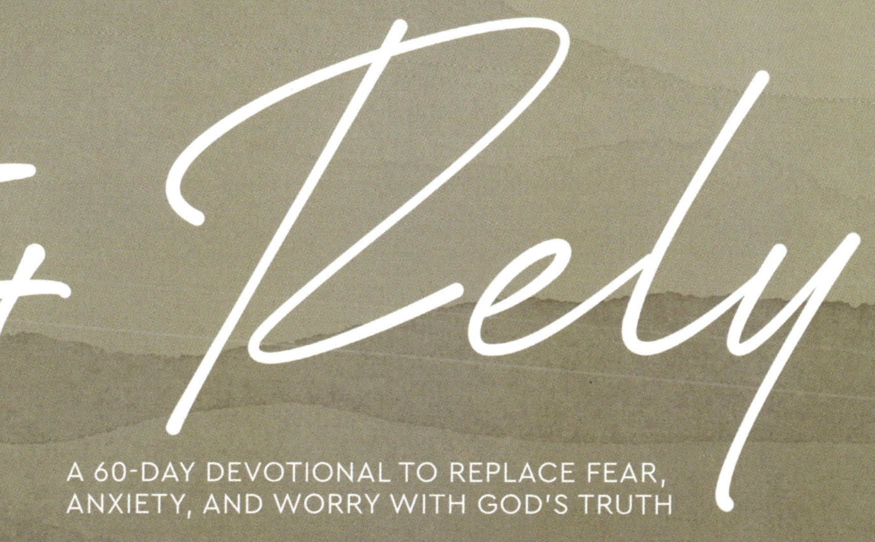

A 60-DAY DEVOTIONAL TO REPLACE FEAR, ANXIETY, AND WORRY WITH GOD'S TRUTH

MADDIE JOY FISCHER

a division of Baker Publishing Group
Grand Rapids, Michigan

Published by Baker Books
a division of Baker Publishing Group
Grand Rapids, Michigan
BakerBooks.com

Printed in China



Library of Congress Cataloging-in-Publication Data
Names: Fischer, Maddie Joy, author.
Title: Rest + rely : a 60-day devotional to replace fear, anxiety, and worry with God's truth / Maddie Joy Fischer.
Other titles: Rest plus rely
Description: Grand Rapids, Michigan : Baker Books, a division of Baker Publishing Group, [2025]
Identifiers: LCCN 2024051219 | ISBN 9781540904010 (cloth) | ISBN 9781493451043 (ebook)
Subjects: LCSH: Young women—Prayers and devotions. | Young women—Religious life. | Anxiety—Religious aspects—Christianity. | Worry—Religious aspects—Christianity. | Devotional literature.
Classification: LCC BV4860 .F597 2025 | DDC 242/.4—dc23/eng/20250109
LC record available at https://lccn.loc.gov/2024051219



Interior design by William Overbeeke

Published in association with Books & Such Literary Management, www.booksandsuch.com

Baker Publishing Group publications use paper produced from sustainable forestry practices and postconsumer waste whenever possible.

25 26 27 28 29 30 31 7 6 5 4 3 2 1

*To my husband, Isaiah.*

The way you love and lead me reflects Jesus.
Thank you for championing me to be
who He has called me to be
and to do what He has called me to do.
It is one of the greatest joys of my life
to love and be loved by you!

# Contents

# INTRODUCTION

## *Unlocking Freedom*

I have been afraid of flying for as long as I can remember. How it works is beyond my understanding, and I find it difficult to trust what I don't understand, especially when said thing is responsible for getting me safely from where I am to where I am going. I think the fear is ultimately rooted in the discomfort of not having control.

Ironically (but not coincidentally), I have had to fly a lot in my lifetime. But I found an article written by a pilot that explains the science and safety of flying—how unlikely it is for anything to go wrong during a flight—and ever since then, it has been much easier for me to get on a plane.

When my understanding of flying increased, I grew more confident in its ability to keep me safe, even though much of it remains beyond my understanding and I still can't fly myself. I think it's safe to say we can compare this to our journey with Jesus.

It's challenging to surrender our lives to a God whose ways are higher than ours. So often, we live held back by fear when

He is calling us to trust Him to get us from where we are—in our comfortability—to where He is calling us. Fear really is a liar and a thief. If we aren't careful, it can cause us to become so consumed by what could go wrong that we miss the abundant life God has for us. If you struggle with fear or anxiety, you are not alone, and you are in the right place. These words were written with you in mind.

I recently polled my Instagram followers and found that 91 percent of participants, out of hundreds, struggle with this every day or most days. I want more for you, for us, and more importantly, God wants and has more for us. I went on to ask the participants what specific fears they face as well as what scriptural truths help them to overcome those fears. I used their responses to assist me in writing this devotional, which is so special to think about.

It's important to understand that freedom from fear is found not only in the knowledge of God's Word but also in trusting what it says and being obedient to what it instructs. Think of the Word as the key to unlocking freedom from fear in your life.

A key is undeniably useful, but it must be used to open the door. The one who uses the key is the one who will be free.

As you read these pages, my hope is that you will experience freedom from fear through a greater understanding of His Word. I pray that the promise of His faithfulness will quiet your fears and settle your heart and mind. I'm not promising you will never feel afraid again but that you will not live consumed or controlled by fear. I pray that as your understanding of who God is grows, your confidence in His ability to get you from where you are to where you are going increases, and that you will step further into the fullness of the abundant life He has for you.

MADDIE JOY

*Day 1*

# THE GOD WHO SEES YOU

But the eyes of the Lord are on those who fear him,
on those whose hope is in his unfailing love.

Psalm 33:18

**ONE OF MY FAVORITE NAMES** for God is El Roi, the God who sees me. He is first described this way in the story of Hagar. Genesis 16:13 says, "Then she called the name of the Lord who spoke to her, 'You are God Who Sees'; for she said, 'Have I not even here [in the wilderness] remained alive after seeing Him [who sees me with understanding and compassion]?'" (AMP).

I would encourage you to take some time to read the whole chapter. Like the servant Hagar who was left alone in the wilderness, we all know what it's like to feel forgotten, overlooked, and unseen. I don't know about you, but I understand wanting to run and hide. There is something profound to take note of here, though. It was when Hagar was hiding in the desert, feeling unseen, that her eyes were opened to view God as the One who

There is *nothing* about your life
that He is unaware of
or that is out of His *control*.

saw her. The New International Version says, "I have now seen the One who sees me." The word now emphasizes the fact that she had not seen God this way before she walked through this hardship. He works similarly in our lives today, by redeeming our pain through a greater revelation of who He is. We only need to open our hearts to what He wants to show us.

I don't know what pain you are experiencing or what fear you are facing today, but I do know that Jesus wants to reveal Himself to you through it, and He will. You are not just known by Him; you are seen with understanding and compassion. There is nothing about your life that He is unaware of or that is out of His control. He will meet you in the middle of your fears and failures and transform them, leaving you with a story to tell of His nearness and goodness.

You are seen.

You are known.

You are understood.

You are unconditionally loved and immeasurably valuable in the eyes of the One who sees you.

> Are not two sparrows sold for a penny? Yet not one of them will fall to the ground outside your Father's care. And even the very hairs of your head are all numbered. So don't be afraid; you are worth more than many sparrows.
>
> **Matthew 10:29–31**

**REFLECTION AND APPLICATION:** What might Jesus want to reveal to you about who He is despite a current fear or pain you are experiencing? How does it help you to know that He is the God who sees you? What fear, anxiety, or worry does the truth from today's devotional replace?

**PRAYER:** Jesus, help me to know that You are the God who sees me with understanding and compassion when I feel unseen. Reveal more of who You are to me as I come to You with my fears, anxieties, and worries. Amen.

## Day 2

# FOR I AM WITH YOU

So do not fear, for I am with you;
do not be dismayed, for I am your God.
I will strengthen you and help you;
I will uphold you with my righteous right hand.

Isaiah 41:10

YOU WILL APPROACH LIFE with a different level of confidence when you know and live in the awareness that you are never alone. The promise that Jesus is not only with us always but that He goes before us is written all throughout Scripture. This means that there is not a fear we face, an unknown we encounter, a failure we experience, an anxious thought we have, or a hardship we are confronted with that God does not meet us in the middle of. He is not absent or careless when it comes to the things that concern us. He is compassionate, understanding, and involved in the details of our lives. He invites us to trust in and rely on Him and promises to never leave or forsake us.

**Only He can take what we dread and turn it around for *good* to reveal His *glory*.**

It's often in the things we beg Him to remove us from or remove from us that we experience His presence and nearness undeniably in our lives. Only He can take what we dread and turn it around for good to reveal His glory.

Knowing that He is near does not mean we will never be afraid, but it helps us to overcome the fears we face rather than live consumed and controlled by them. Because of His nearness, help, and strength, we can experience victory over what would otherwise destroy us. With His Word as our weapon and His truth as our guide, we can walk in freedom from anything that attempts to hinder us.

Instead of praying for fear to be eliminated from your life altogether, ask for eyes to see it as an opportunity to grow in your understanding of and confidence in the One who walks with you.

Because He is with you, for you, and never fails you, fear does not have the final say over your life. The truth of His Word does.

> And surely I am with you always, to the very end of the age.
>
> **Matthew 28:20**

**REFLECTION AND APPLICATION:** How does knowing that Jesus is always with you change your perspective about the uncertainties you face? What fear, anxiety, or worry does the truth from today's devotional replace?

**PRAYER:** Jesus, my hope is in the promise that You are always with me. Remind me when I feel alone in my fears that You will never leave me or forsake me. Amen.

*Day 3*

# WRESTLING WITH WHAT-IFS

Jesus answered, "It is written: 'Man shall not live on bread alone, but on every word that comes from the mouth of God.'"

Matthew 4:4

THE WHAT-IFS AND IF-ONLYS that fill our minds can be unending and consuming.

What if this happens?

What if that happens?

What if this or that doesn't happen?

If only this would happen . . .

If only that would happen . . .

If only they would do this or that . . .

Then life might be easier, or I might feel more in control, or I would at least feel more predictable or safe.

Sound familiar? Fill in the blank with anything else your own internal dialogue might say. The truth is, we are quick to place our hope in possibilities and quick to be defeated by uncertainties. We need to be continually reminded that God's promises are greater than our possibilities, and they uplift us in our greatest defeats. They are an anchor in the storms we face and our confidence in uncertainty.

Release the what-ifs and if-onlys on your mind (finances, friendships, the future, etc.) into His mighty hands because He alone can be trusted with them. He is not only aware of your every need, but He knows every dream and desire in your heart. He sees the certainties beyond the maybes and is orchestrating your life from a view of the full picture while your view is limited.

Instead of dwelling on and being consumed by the unknowns that fill your mind, live according to the "IT IS WRITTEN" of His Word daily. Establish His Word as your standard and guide. Instead of trying to take matters into your own hands, leave the orchestrating in the hands of the One whose plans for you are good and will prevail. Confidence in the unchanging truth of His Word is the only place where true security and fulfillment will be found in this lifetime.

Have confidence in what He has spoken. Live according to the "it is written."

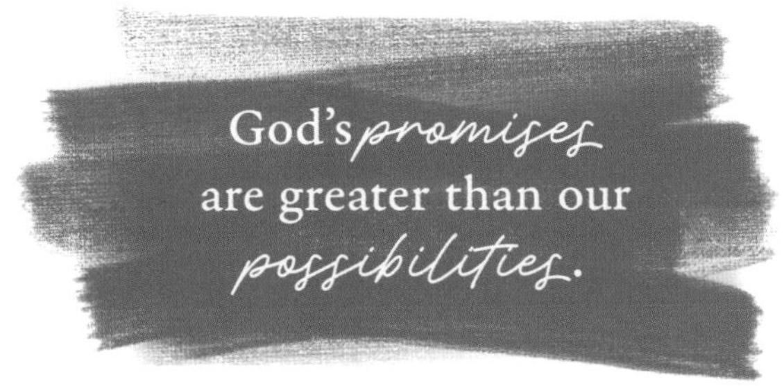

Settle your heart and mind on His promises, which are reliable and true. The what-ifs will leave you wondering. He never will.

> The grass withers and the flowers fade,
> but the word of our God stands forever.
> **Isaiah 40:8 NLT**

**REFLECTION AND APPLICATION:** What "what-if" or "if-only" thoughts do you need to replace with an "it is written" mindset? What fear, anxiety, or worry does the truth from today's devotional replace?

**PRAYER:** Jesus, thank You for Your Word, which always proves true. Guide me in living according to the "it is writtens" when I am consumed by what-ifs and if-onlys. Amen.

*Day 4*

# EVERY THOUGHT CAPTIVE

> We demolish arguments and every pretension that sets itself up against the knowledge of God, and we take captive every thought to make it obedient to Christ.
>
> 2 Corinthians 10:5

ONE OF THE MOST detrimental things to our faith is to walk through life numb to or unaware of the authority over fear we have been given through Jesus.

Imagine someone being freed from prison because the price for their bail has been paid, but they choose to remain a prisoner. This concept is hard for us to comprehend because it isn't our current reality, but maybe it is more than we realize in a spiritual sense. The price for our freedom from sin and all its effects has been paid in full by the blood of Jesus, yet we often choose to remain captive to the things He died to save and free us from.

It's one thing to be free; it's another to live in freedom. The hope and plan of our Savior is for us to walk continually in freedom

Live every moment in the *fullness* of *freedom* Christ died for you to have.

from fear and anything else holding us captive, even our own thoughts. Thankfully, Scripture instructs us on how to handle thoughts that don't align with the truth of His Word. It says to "take captive every thought to make it obedient to Christ" (2 Cor. 10:5). Not some thoughts. Every thought. It seems like an impossible task, but nothing is impossible with the help of His power at work within us.

We can't take our thoughts captive and submit them to the obedience of a truth that we don't know. Living a life of freedom from fear requires that we grow continually in the knowledge and understanding of the only truth that delivers. Then we must apply and live out the truth in our thoughts, words, and actions.

You have victory over fear because of the authority you have been given in Jesus. Don't just know that you are free; live every moment in the fullness of freedom Christ died for you to have.

> It is for freedom that Christ has set us free. Stand firm, then, and do not let yourselves be burdened again by a yoke of slavery.
>
> **Galatians 5:1**

**REFLECTION AND APPLICATION:** In what way(s) are you living bound instead of in the freedom Christ died for you to have? What thoughts or emotions do you need to take captive and make obedient to Christ? What fear, anxiety, or worry does the truth from today's devotional replace?

**PRAYER:** Jesus, increase my awareness of the authority You have given me over fear and anxiety. Show me what thoughts I need to take captive and make obedient to what Your Word says. Amen.

*Day 5*

# LIGHT + SALVATION

The LORD is my light and my salvation;
  whom shall I fear?
The LORD is the stronghold of my life;
  of whom shall I be afraid?
Psalm 27:1 ESV

THE MORE WE LOOK at who Jesus is, the less consuming fear becomes. In Psalm 27, David describes Jesus as these three things in the face of fear:

**#1: Jesus is our light.**

Have you ever noticed that there is something about the night that makes everything more unsettling? Everything changes when the sun comes up. There is clarity. There is levity. That is the significance of Jesus being described as our light. He is the sun that shines through our fears that feel dark and scary. His light leads us when we're unsure where to go or what to do next.

**#2: Jesus is our salvation.**

Since He is our salvation, our future as His people is secure. Because of His deliverance, we are saved from the punishment that we deserve, a life separated from Him. This truth is something to celebrate, not just every day but every moment. It is the greatest gift ever given and the hope of our lives forever.

**#3: Jesus is the stronghold of our lives.**

Psalm 91:2 says that He is our refuge and fortress (NIV). While circumstances all around us are constantly shifting, Jesus remains a constant stronghold. In the face of fear, we have a fortress, a place of safety, to run to and rely on. When life is heavy and hard, we have an unwavering hope to hold on to, because He is holding on to us and will never let go.

Victory over fear and anxiety is not achieved in our own strength but through a life of confident trust in Jesus as our light, salvation, and stronghold. We will be provided with many

Victory over fear and anxiety is not achieved in our own *strength* but through a life of confident *trust* in Jesus.

reasons to fear throughout our lives, but we have been given a more powerful reason not to fear in the unchanging promise of who our Savior is.

> Jesus spoke to the people once more and said, "I am the light of the world. If you follow me, you won't have to walk in darkness, because you will have the light that leads to life."
>
> **John 8:12 NLT**

**REFLECTION AND APPLICATION:** How do the truths in Psalm 27:1 about who Jesus is (our light, salvation, and stronghold) give you hope in the current fears you are facing? What fear, anxiety, or worry does the truth from today's devotional replace?

**PRAYER:** Jesus, lead me to run to You as my refuge and rely on You as my strength in every circumstance. I have nothing to fear because You are my light, salvation, and stronghold. Amen.

*Day 6*

# BULLIED BY A SHADOW

You came near when I called you,
and you said, "Do not fear."
Lamentations 3:57

I HAVE FOUND FEAR to be like a shadow of something that appears larger than it is. Fear and anxiety have a way of distorting reality to make what is in front of us feel all-consuming. I remember the Holy Spirit once whispering so gently to my heart to no longer live my life bullied by the shadow of fear but to set up camp in the confidence of God's truth. There is nothing wrong with acknowledging fear; the problem happens when we give fear authority in our lives over the truth of His Word.

Fear won't flee by ignoring it or trying harder to overcome it in your own strength. You must instead allow the light of Jesus to shine into the shadows of fear surrounding you. Freedom from fear takes place when you allow His love to consume the fears that have consumed you.

There is nothing wrong with *acknowledging* fear; the problem happens when we give fear *authority* in our lives over the truth of His Word.

In 1 John 4:18, we learn that His perfect love casts out all fear. So allow His love to invade even your deepest fears. Stop living bullied by the shadow of fear. Face it with confidence, not in your own power but in His. This is easier said than lived, but nothing is impossible with God's help.

Here are three truths to help you experience victory over fear:

**#1 Fear is loud. His voice is louder.**

When you are familiar with God's voice, you will be able to identify even His softest whisper over the roar of fear. As loud and scary as fear may sound, His voice will be your guide and lead you to freedom and peace. "My sheep listen to my voice; I know them, and they follow me" (John 10:27).

**#2 Fear is powerful. He is all-powerful.**

Fear is powerful and persuasive, but only God has ultimate authority. It's okay to acknowledge fear, but always return to the promise of His sovereignty. His Word has authority over every fear. Use His Word as your weapon, and you will walk in victory. "Now Christ has gone to heaven. He is seated in the place of honor next to God, and all the angels and authorities and powers accept his authority" (1 Pet. 3:22 NLT).

**#3 Fear has a lot to say. He has the final say.**

Fear will tell you many things. It will fill you with concerns, confusion, and doubt. Despite how fear might make you feel, decide that you will not allow what contradicts His Word to direct you. His Word is unchanging, unfailing, and has the final say. Walking in His way leads to life. "Then Jesus came to them and said, 'All authority in heaven and on earth has been given to me'" (Matt. 28:18).

> So we say with confidence,
>
> "The Lord is my helper; I will not be afraid.
> What can mere mortals do to me?"
>
> **Hebrews 13:6**

**REFLECTION AND APPLICATION:** Which of these three truths resonates with you most right now? Why? What fear, anxiety, or worry does the truth from today's devotional replace?

**PRAYER:** Jesus, I invite You to shine Your light on the dark shadows of fear that have consumed me. I establish Your Word as the ultimate authority in my life. Amen.

*Day 7*

# OPPORTUNITY IN THE UNKNOWN

Have you never heard?
  Have you never understood?
The Lord is the everlasting God,
  the Creator of all the earth.
He never grows weak or weary.
  No one can measure the depths of his
    understanding.

Isaiah 40:28 NLT

I DON'T KNOW ABOUT YOU, but the unknown, waiting, and in-between are all things I dread. My dread for these things or even my attempts to run from or avoid them have never changed the reality that I continue to face them. These things are inevitable and are mostly unpredictable parts of life. You and I don't know everything, and we don't always know what is coming next.

Over time, I have arrived at the realization that God has a way of using the things that are out of my control to remind me of my need for Him. In my uncertainty, He is the only thing I can remain certain of. Over time, the unknown in your life will increase your trust in Jesus if you turn to Him in the face of uncertainty and simply choose to follow Him. The unknown will increase your confidence as you give Him opportunities to prove His faithfulness. The waiting produces patience and keeps you dependent on Him.

I am no expert. I still struggle in the tension of uncertainty. But I have learned to at least dread less what increases my dependence on Jesus. I have learned to ask Him to help me see circumstances through spiritual eyes. I have learned to stand on the promise that He delights in the details of my life and knows what is coming, even when I am unsure. In the unknown, I get to see the evidence of His faithfulness in ways I don't experience when I do know what is coming.

I don't know everything, but I know the One who does, and He calls me by name.

That is where my confidence is found. Dare I say that because of these realities, there is peace, expectation, and even

God has a way of *using* the things
that are out of my control
to *remind* me of my need for Him.

excitement to be found in the face of the unknown. He is leading us through and growing our confidence in and dependence on Him along the way. It's a gift! May we see it as such.

> Show me your ways, Lord,
>     teach me your paths.
> Guide me in your truth and teach me,
>     for you are God my Savior,
>     and my hope is in you all day long.
>
> **Psalm 25:4–5**

**REFLECTION AND APPLICATION:** Identify an unknown or uncertainty you are currently facing. How is it an opportunity to grow your trust in Jesus? What fear, anxiety, or worry does the truth from today's devotional replace?

**PRAYER:** Jesus, I want to see the unknown as an opportunity to trust You. Fill me with peace, expectation, and excitement for what is to come. Amen.

*Day 8*

# GUIDE

> I will instruct you and teach you in the way you
> should go;
> I will counsel you with my loving eye on you.
>
> Psalm 32:8

I HAVE FOUND THAT ANXIETY is often a result of my trying to control what I am called to surrender to Jesus. A good example of this is when I try to orchestrate or order my own steps where Scripture says that Jesus is my guide and my Good Shepherd. I am not saying there is anything wrong with having a plan, but those plans should be submitted to His authority. We are not called or created to be the orderer of our own steps or the determiner of our own days. We are called to be followers (or disciples) of Jesus. He goes before us and instructs us accordingly.

Instead of living consumed and overwhelmed in an attempt to formulate and carry out your plan and see your desires come to pass, live in pursuit of the Good Shepherd. Doing things your own way leads to frustration; submission to His way leads to

**Doing things your own way leads to *frustration*; submission to His way leads to *fulfillment*.**

fulfillment. Get to know His plans for you, which are for your good and His glory. Knowing Him more is always better than knowing what steps to take next.

This is why He often leads us through hardships instead of out of them. He values what the process—and at times pain—produces within us. His strength and power are revealed through our weakness.

Run to Him instead of from Him. Your confidence in His guidance will help you overcome fear of failure, the unknown, missing out, and lack. It doesn't mean it will be easy, but it does mean He will see you through. Move forward in the promise that He is with you and for you until the end of time.

He is the greatest guide.

> The heart of man plans his way,
> but the Lord establishes his steps.
> **Proverbs 16:9 ESV**
>
> He renews my strength.
> He guides me along right paths,
> bringing honor to his name.
> **Psalm 23:3 NLT**

**REFLECTION AND APPLICATION:** Where have you tried to control what you are called to surrender? Why should you spend more time in pursuit of Jesus than planning your own way? What fear, anxiety, or worry does the truth from today's devotional replace?

**PRAYER:** Jesus, thank You for being my Good Shepherd and the greatest guide. Help me to trust Your leadership in every area of my life and to prioritize pursuing You over anything else. Amen.

## *Day 9*

# FORGIVEN

> If we confess our sins, he is faithful and just and will forgive us our sins and purify us from all unrighteousness.
>
> 1 John 1:9

**YOUR PAST HAS THE POWER** to hinder you from experiencing the future Jesus has for you only if you give it the authority. When you repent (turn away from your wrongdoing against Him), He is quick to forgive. Not only does He forgive, but Jeremiah 31:34 tells us that He gladly forgets the sins that separate us from Him. This is so important to remember when you fear that you can't be used because of your past.

Psalm 103:12 says, "He has removed our sins as far from us as the east is from the west" (NLT).

You are not disqualified because of what you did last year, last month, or even last night. In fact, your past is an opportunity for His redemptive work to be displayed for those around you to see. Your weakness reveals His strength, and your imperfection points to the only One who is without flaw. He is the only

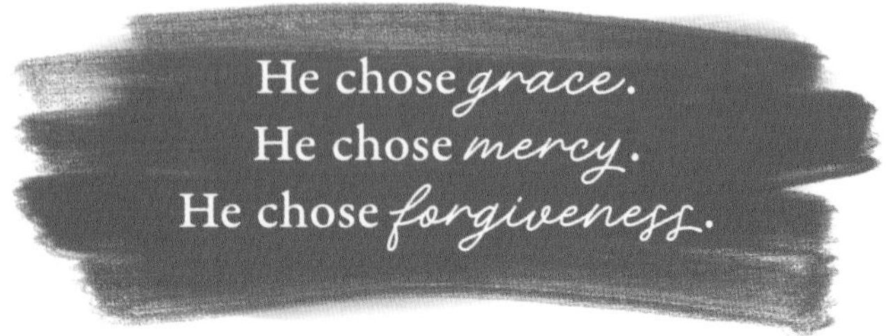


One who can disqualify you because of your sin, but instead, He chose the cross.

He chose grace. He chose mercy. He chose forgiveness.

Because of His choice, you are no longer defined by what you have done, by your fears, or by your failures. Simply accepting His salvation and surrendering your life to His way redefines who you are and whose you are. When you give your life to Jesus, you truly become a new creation in Him. You may have heard this many times but still find yourself struggling to live like it's true. He wants to help you.

Where we hold grudges, He extends grace upon grace.

Where we see failure, He sees the finished work of the cross.

Where we see a broken past, He sees a future full of hope and restoration.

Your past may be a part of your story, but there is no brokenness that is beyond His ability to redeem. Forgive (yourself and others) like He has forgiven you, and walk in the new identity you have been given in Him!

Despite your past, you are full of purpose. Don't dwell on what has been forgiven and forgotten today. Walk in freedom.

> Therefore, if anyone is in Christ, the new creation has come: The old has gone, the new is here!
>
> **2 Corinthians 5:17**

**REFLECTION AND APPLICATION:** Why is it difficult to accept Jesus's forgiveness? In what area of your life do you need to forget what He has already forgiven and step into the future He has for you? What fear, anxiety, or worry does the truth from today's devotional replace?

**PRAYER:** Jesus, thank You for choosing forgiveness so that I can walk in freedom. Help me to forget what You have forgiven so that I can walk in the newness of life I have in You. Amen.

*Day 10*

# REST

> Then Jesus said, "Come to me, all of you who are weary and carry heavy burdens, and I will give you rest. Take my yoke upon you. Let me teach you, because I am humble and gentle at heart, and you will find rest for your souls."
>
> Matthew 11:28–29 NLT

**TO REST** means to be based on or grounded in; to depend on or to place hope, trust, or confidence on or in.

Today, instead of orchestrating your own plans, yield to Jesus's way.

Instead of panicking, pray.

Instead of rushing, rest in Him.

Instead of striving, surrender.

Instead of relying on self, rely on Him.

You are called and created for more than a life filled with hurry and worry, but that "more" will require you to submit your life to a rhythm of rest in Jesus through trust in and obedience to His Word. To trade restlessness for rest, you must depend on His leadership in your life. It's hard to trust someone you don't

He will lift your *heavy* burdens and *hold* you up.

know personally. Get to know your Good Shepherd more each day. Don't neglect time with Him in the secret place. Through that intentional time, He will increase your confidence in His promises to guide, provide for, and protect you. When you put your life in His hands, choosing to believe that He will be faithful to His Word, you exchange your heavy load for His burden, which is light.

Live a life of continual reliance on Jesus. Rest in the peace that trusting in Him provides. Stand on and be grounded in His Word. Live dependent on His faithfulness. Place your hope and confidence in Him in every circumstance and situation. He will lift your heavy burdens and hold you up. He will renew your strength and sustain you when you are unsure of how to move forward.

Accept His invitation to continually come to Him. Live in the comfort of dwelling with Him. In His presence, there is rest for your soul. In His presence, there is fullness of joy. In His presence, there is perfect peace.

> The Lord replied, "My Presence will go with you, and I will give you rest."
>
> **Exodus 33:14**

**REFLECTION AND APPLICATION:** How does your life reveal whether you are resting in Jesus? What heavy burden are you carrying that you need to exchange for His light burden? What fear, anxiety, or worry does the truth from today's devotional replace?

**PRAYER:** Jesus, thank You that in Your presence there is perfect peace. I choose to exchange restlessness and hurry for true rest in You. Amen.

## *Day 11*

# SEEK

> *When You said*, "Seek My face [in prayer, require My presence as your greatest need]," my heart said to You, "Your face, O LORD, I will seek [on the authority of Your word]."
>
> Psalm 27:8 AMP

COULD IT BE that our restlessness and lack of satisfaction in life is a result of our disobedience to God's instruction to seek Him first?

God's people tend to complicate what He has made simple. At the cost of our peace, we are easily distracted by the pursuit of lesser things when He has told us to put Him first. One of the most beautiful things about God's presence is that it is not limited to specific places or perfect moments in our lives. He is always near and always available, so we can continually dwell in Him. We are called to abide in Him—our light, our salvation, our refuge and fortress.

"Seek Him first" is not a cliché; it is an instruction spoken with intention, which leads to a life of true fulfillment and satisfaction. Seeking Him should not be viewed as an obligation to God but

**Live in *obedience* to His command to seek Him first, for He is where *peace*, *purpose*, and *joy* are found.**

as an honor and opportunity to grow in our knowledge and understanding of Him.

I have recently asked myself these questions and would challenge you to do the same: What have I desired more than His presence? What have I sought more than His face?

Then, ask Him to tear down those idols in your life and return you again and again to the simple and sincere pursuit of Him above all else.

His presence is more important than anything else that desires your attention. Pursuing Him first will cause the rest to unravel according to His perfect plan and purpose for your life.

Our lives should reveal that He is both our greatest need and desire. Live in obedience to His command to seek Him first, for He is where peace, purpose, and joy are found.

> Look to the Lord and his strength;
> seek his face always.
> **1 Chronicles 16:11**

**REFLECTION AND APPLICATION:** Why is it important to seek Jesus first? What (if anything) have you put before seeking Him? What fear, anxiety, or worry does the truth from today's devotional replace?

**PRAYER:** Jesus, help me to seek You before anyone and anything else. Let my life be evidence that You are both my greatest need and desire. Amen.

## *Day 12*

# FAITHFUL FULFILLER

> The Lord isn't really being slow about his promise, as some people think. No, he is being patient for your sake. He does not want anyone to be destroyed, but wants everyone to repent.
>
> 2 Peter 3:9 NLT

WHAT DO YOU DO when what you see seems to contradict what God has promised? What do you do when discouragement creeps in and whispers the lie that, surely, He has forgotten what He has spoken?

First, remember He is God and He is sovereign. Move forward in remembrance of who He is and what He has done. Recount His faithfulness and choose to praise. It's not just what He has done that makes Him worthy of our worship but who He is. The promise of His sovereignty does not diminish our feelings or the challenges we face, but it does give us a sustaining hope through the trials and uncertainties we experience in this life. He has the authority and the final say.

Second, understand that God is perfect (unfailing) in faithfulness. As people who frequently fail and are frequently failed by others, it's challenging to wrap our minds around someone being perfect in nature. This is why it's easy to find ourselves fearful that God won't follow through, especially when the fulfillment of His promise doesn't arrive when or how we hoped or expected. He is not slow to keep His promise as it may at times seem; He is working according to His perfect plan and process, which we will not always understand.

This is where faith comes in—faith to trust that He will follow through with what He has spoken regardless of the time that passes and things that happen between what is promised and the fulfillment of the promise. You don't have to hold your breath wondering if He will be faithful when it comes to your life. You can be confident and sure that He will. His failure to follow through will not begin with you because He cannot fail.

He will fulfill His every promise. Expect to see and experience the faithfulness of Jesus in your life. He will not only meet your

He will fulfill His every *promise*. Expect to see and experience the *faithfulness* of Jesus in your life.

expectations, but He will far exceed them, even when it looks different than what you had in mind.

> Lord, you are my God;
> I will exalt you and praise your name,
> for in perfect faithfulness
> you have done wonderful things,
> things planned long ago.
>
> **Isaiah 25:1**

**REFLECTION AND APPLICATION:** How does God's Word instruct you to respond when you fear that He won't be faithful? In what situation or circumstance can you apply this instruction? What fear, anxiety, or worry does the truth from today's devotional replace?

**PRAYER:** Jesus, I rest in the promise that You fulfill every promise You make. Help me to live in continual expectation of Your faithfulness. Amen.

*Day 13*

# WHEN GOD SEEMS SILENT

> The LORD is near to all who call on him,
> to all who call on him in truth.
>
> Psalm 145:18

SOME OF THE BEST friendships are the ones where you can be in each other's presence for an extended amount of time but not have to say a word. That comfortability in silence speaks to the intimacy of those relationships; there is no expectation to host, perform, or entertain but to simply be together. The silence isn't uncomfortable; it's safe. The silence doesn't cause feelings of distance; it speaks to the closeness of the friendship.

With that said, as believers, Jesus should be our closest friend. I think about the times I find myself frustrated and discouraged and unable to hear His voice and, I don't know about you, I tend to correlate His silence with Him being distant or uninvolved. I find myself feeling fearful and lonely when He is not speaking to me as clearly or as often as He has in other times in my life.

When you struggle to hear His *voice*, trust His *heart*.

So how should we respond when Jesus seems silent? Let's look to His Word. In Psalm 139, we see this promise that we cannot escape His presence:

> Where shall I go from your Spirit?
> Or where shall I flee from your presence?
> If I ascend to heaven, you are there!
> If I make my bed in Sheol, you are there!
> If I take the wings of the morning
> and dwell in the uttermost parts of the sea,
> even there your hand shall lead me,
> and your right hand shall hold me.
>
> vv. 7–10 ESV

Jesus's seeming silence does not mean He is distant or uninvolved in our lives. His presence is always available to us. When God seems silent, we have the promise of His nearness to cling to. When you struggle to hear His voice, trust His heart. Continue to call on Him with confidence that He hears you and will not abandon you in your time of need. Take the opportunity to simply be in the presence of your closest friend. He is near, and He is working beyond what you can currently see.

> If we are faithless,
> he remains faithful,
> for he cannot disown himself.
> **2 Timothy 2:13**

**REFLECTION AND APPLICATION:** How does knowing that Jesus is near help when He seems silent? Why is it important to take time to simply be in His presence? What fear, anxiety, or worry does the truth from today's devotional replace?

**PRAYER:** Jesus, I know that You are always near and that You hear me when I call. When You seem silent, help me to hold on to the promise of Your nearness. Amen.

*Day 14*

# REMEMBRANCE

> I will [solemnly] remember the deeds of the Lord;
> Yes, I will [wholeheartedly] remember Your
> wonders of old.
>
> Psalm 77:11 AMP

A LIFE CONSUMED with earthly concerns can quickly lead to a life defined by a constant state of restlessness. Restlessness is a lack of rest caused by anxiety. If you are anything like me, you may sometimes feel trapped in a never-ending cycle of fear and having to figure out what is next. In an attempt to keep everything under control, you don't let yourself slow down but still feel like you can't keep up. You know that this is not the abundance God has for you, but you don't know how to break the cycle, so you feel stuck, frustrated, and maybe even ashamed.

I want to encourage you that there is an answer, and it might be simpler than you think. A good place to start is remembrance. Life will always be full of things that are out of our control and that we cannot change. There will always be things to do, decisions to make, and disappointments to face. We can't run from those realities, but we can always return to this unchanging promise in the face of them—the promise of Jesus's faithfulness and involvement in the details of our lives. I have found that restlessness is often the result of attempting to take matters into my own hands instead of placing them into the hands of the One whose faithfulness never fails.

Surrendering control does not mean we are exempt from responsibility, but it does mean we don't have to carry the weight of life's heavy load alone. It allows us to slow down, find rest, and be sustained by God's strength when ours runs out.

Remembrance is one of the best remedies for restlessness. All throughout Scripture, we see invitations to remember who God is and what He has done in moments of fear and overwhelm. Remembrance helps reconnect us to our source when we have grown doubtful or disconnected. Recalling His faithfulness allows us to see our earthly concerns through the lens of eternity. While it does not make hardships nonexistent or eliminate every challenge, it does make them far less consuming.

Build intentional moments of remembrance into your everyday life. Living aware of the goodness of Jesus will change your worry to worship, your concern to confidence, and your restlessness to rest in Him alone.

Recalling His *faithfulness* allows us to see our earthly concerns through the lens of *eternity*.

> Let all that I am praise the Lord;
> may I never forget the good things he does for me.
> **Psalm 103:2 NLT**

**REFLECTION AND APPLICATION:** What are you restless or anxious about? How does remembering the faithfulness of Jesus change your perspective? What fear, anxiety, or worry does the truth from today's devotional replace?

**PRAYER:** Jesus, I accept Your invitation to live a life focused on remembering who You are and what You have done. Increase my confidence in Your faithfulness through moments of remembrance. Amen.

*Day 15*

# CALM IN CHAOS

> The mind governed by the flesh is death, but the mind governed by the Spirit is life and peace.
>
> Romans 8:6

HAVE YOU EVER WONDERED if our hearts and minds feel so chaotic because we have allowed far too many opinions into them? Actually, for many of us, I am certain that's exactly why.

We are not created to receive the amount of information and advice constantly bombarding us in today's culture, not even if it's useful information. We open our devices daily to hundreds of thousands of conflicting opinions on who we should be, how we should live, and what we should do, say, wear, eat, share, and believe. While it's not all bad information, it can quickly lead to conflict, comparison, chaos, and overwhelm in our hearts and minds as we attempt to keep up with it all. No wonder we find ourselves anxious and insecure.

The good news is that we are not called to keep up with anyone's standard but the word of the One who created us. He calls

In Him *alone*, your soul can truly find rest, satisfaction, and security.

us to rest in Him, and He calls us out of the pressure of rushing to keep up with everyone else's opinion.

His guidance and the sound of His voice are our calm in the chaos of all the other voices shouting around us. Know His voice, the voice of truth, and His Word better than you know anything else. Filter every opinion and piece of advice through the standard of His Word and His guidance. Be in His presence far more than you scroll on your phone or mindlessly do other things that will not give you peace but rob you of it.

As long as you search for satisfaction and fulfillment outside of the Prince of Peace, you will never find it. Follow Him. Ask Him to continually remind you of who you are and what He is calling you to do, and then stay in that lane.

In Him alone, your soul can truly find rest, satisfaction, and security in a chaotic world where everyone is being pulled in every direction. Fix your eyes on Jesus and follow the sound of His voice.

> Set your minds on things above, not on earthly things.
> **Colossians 3:2**

**REFLECTION AND APPLICATION:** Who or what have you listened to over the sound of Jesus's voice? Where have you struggled with keeping up with the world's way of doing things where He is calling you to submit to the standard of His Word? What fear, anxiety, or worry does the truth from today's devotional replace?

**PRAYER:** Jesus, thank You for being the calm in chaos. As I spend time in Your presence, teach me to identify and follow the sound of Your voice over all the other noises that surround me. Amen.

*Day 16*

# CERTAIN OF HIS SOVEREIGNTY

The Lord has established his throne in heaven,
and his kingdom rules over all.

Psalm 103:19

I WAS RECENTLY TALKING to a friend who is walking through deep pain. The only encouragement I could provide was to listen and gently remind her of who God is. I don't know or understand why she is walking through what she is walking through, and I can't fix it for her. If I could, I would take away the pain she is feeling in a heartbeat. But, despite the things I don't know, I do know that God is sovereign. Although sometimes I think I know better, I recognize that the weight of the world is far better off in the palms of Jesus's nail-scarred hands than in mine.

It's important to understand that His sovereignty does not invalidate our pain; it gives us hope in our deepest pain and in our darkest moments.

> The *weight* of the world is far better off in the palms of Jesus's nail-scarred *hands* than in mine.

His sovereignty does not minimize our feelings and fears; it guides us in navigating them and anchors us in truth when we are swayed by the things of the world.

His sovereignty is not a passive or dismissive approach or solution; it is the answer to our uncertainties.

When our words fail or fall short, His never do.

When we lack the answer or solution, He always knows what to say and do.

When everything is out of our control and feels like it's falling apart, it is never out of His reach or ability to turn things around for good. He holds all things together in His hands.

As Colossians 1:17 reminds us, "He is before all things, and in him all things hold together."

I don't know what you are walking through, but God does, and He knows exactly what you need. If I could take the pain that you are facing away, I would. But know that the Healer knows you by name. He has the world, including your little world, in His hands. You may not understand, but you can trust that He knows best and is working on your behalf. Rest in the promise of His sovereignty. Let it comfort you during your deepest pain, in your darkest moment, and through every unknown.

> I make known the end from the beginning,
> from ancient times, what is still to come.
> I say, "My purpose will stand,
> and I will do all that I please."
>
> **Isaiah 46:10**

**REFLECTION AND APPLICATION:** How does the awareness of God's sovereignty comfort you in the face of uncertainty? What fear, anxiety, or worry does the truth from today's devotional replace?

**PRAYER:** Jesus, I desire to live in the peace provided with trusting that nothing is out of Your control. Point me to the promise of Your sovereignty in every situation. Amen.

*Day 17*

# FACING CHANGE

> The LORD himself goes before you and will be with you; he will never leave you nor forsake you. Do not be afraid; do not be discouraged.
>
> Deuteronomy 31:8

I CANNOT EMPHASIZE ENOUGH that it is okay to feel afraid. However, it is not God's plan for us to allow fear to hinder us from moving forward into what He has prepared for us.

Life changes and we can't stop it from happening no matter how hard we try.

I have always struggled with change and transition. I want to hold on to comfort as much as I can, but some of the most rewarding things require a level of discomfort. The more you step out and follow God's guidance, the more you will grow in boldness and confidence to be who He has called you to be and to do what He has called you to do.

Ask Him to help you decide that you would rather be uncomfortable than grow complacent. After all, complacency is far more dangerous than many of the things we are afraid of. It keeps us

*Complacency* is far more dangerous than many of the things we are *afraid* of.

stuck. I often combat fear of change by reminding myself that I have two choices: to move forward in the face of fear or to wonder what would happen if I did.

What is scarier to me than facing fear is the thought of looking back in regret and wishing I would have followed God's lead. You have this one life to live—it's too precious to allow fear to hinder you from the abundance of what God has planned and prepared for you.

But you might be facing a change that is out of your control or that you did not get to choose, and it has left you feeling disoriented and confused. If that is where you find yourself, I pray your heart finds rest in the confidence that the One who goes before you saw this coming long before you did. As you are forced to face what you would not have chosen, I pray you put your hope in Him and don't let go. He is your constant and He is always with you.

> For I am the Lord your God
> who takes hold of your right hand
> and says to you, Do not fear;
> I will help you.
>
> **Isaiah 41:13**

**REFLECTION AND APPLICATION:** Why is change unsettling? How does the promise that God is constant provide peace in a life that is constantly changing? What fear, anxiety, or worry does the truth from today's devotional replace?

**PRAYER:** Jesus, thank You for being constant no matter what changes in my life. Help me to move forward in confidence in You even when I am afraid of the unknown. Amen.

*Day 18*

# A CALL TO COURAGE

Be strong and courageous. Do not be afraid or terrified because of them, for the LORD your God goes with you; he will never leave you nor forsake you.

Deuteronomy 31:6

COURAGE IS NOT a suggestion but a command given to those who follow Jesus. We are not commanded to never be afraid but to be more confident in the One who is always with us than whatever we come up against. Living a truly courageous life is only possible through confidence in Jesus. He is the only One greater than everything. He is the only One who can do all things.

Joshua 1:9 is one of the most well-known Scriptures. It says, "Have I not commanded you? Be strong and courageous. Do not be afraid; do not be discouraged, for the LORD your God will be with you wherever you go."

Living a truly *courageous* life is only possible through *confidence* in Jesus.

It's simple to quote but challenging to live. When God commanded Joshua to be courageous in his calling, He did not suggest that there would be nothing to fear, but He promised to be with Joshua wherever He went. He guaranteed that Joshua would never face challenges alone. And God never makes a promise that He won't keep.

I believe that Jesus is calling you, like He called Joshua, to be courageous. It's important to recognize that you can only walk in that calling if you have confidence in Him. Your own strength and might will eventually fail you.

Since He is with you wherever you go, you can live a life of courage, even when you feel anything but courageous. You have everything you need to step into all that He has called and instructed you to do, but you must choose to continually step forward in obedience even when you don't feel courageous.

> Wait patiently for the Lord.
> Be brave and courageous.
> Yes, wait patiently for the Lord.
> **Psalm 27:14 NLT**

**REFLECTION AND APPLICATION:** Why does God call you to things you can't do in your own strength? How can you be courageous when you don't feel courageous? What fear, anxiety, or worry does the truth from today's devotional replace?

**PRAYER:** Jesus, I accept Your call to be courageous. I know this can be accomplished only through confidence in You. When I am afraid, remind me that You are with me wherever I go and that I am equipped through You to do what You have called me to do. Amen.

*Day 19*

# THINK ON THESE THINGS

> And now, dear brothers and sisters, one final thing. Fix your thoughts on what is true, and honorable, and right, and pure, and lovely, and admirable. Think about things that are excellent and worthy of praise.
>
> Philippians 4:8 NLT

GOD'S WORD is available to us, but we have to choose whether we apply it and live like it is true. We choose whether to build our confidence in what He has spoken or let fear dictate our decision-making and decide our future, but we can't choose both paths.

What will you dwell on? I believe that your answer to this question will determine your days on earth.

Will you dwell on your doubts or His promises?

Will you dwell on what you see or what He said?

Will you dwell on fear or truth?

Will you dwell on people's opinions or God's opinion?

Will you dwell on what's out of your control or the promise of His sovereignty?

Will you dwell on your thoughts and feelings or His promises?

Our thoughts are powerful. If you focus on what is fleeting and falling apart, you will spend your days consumed by fear, anxiety, and overwhelm. The good news is that there is a better option! If you dwell on His Word, which lasts forever, you will walk in the freedom, peace, and joy it provides and produces within you.

What you think about matters, so fill your mind with good thoughts. Dwell on an unchanging, unfailing God and His unchanging, unfailing Word. Draw near to Him daily. Set up camp in the confidence that He will be faithful—always and every time. Give His truth the authority to dictate your future instead of giving power to your fleeting feelings and fears.

When you decide to be obedient to what His Word instructs regarding your thoughts, you will experience the abundance He has for you.

> You will keep in perfect peace
> all who trust in you,
> all whose thoughts are fixed on you!
> **Isaiah 26:3 NLT**

**Dwell on an *unchanging*, unfailing God and His unchanging, *unfailing* Word.**

**REFLECTION AND APPLICATION:** Are your thoughts currently producing fear or peace? If your answer is fear, write down a list of thoughts that will lead to peace using Philippians 4:8 as a guide. What fear, anxiety, or worry does the truth from today's devotional replace?

**PRAYER:** Jesus, thank You for Your instruction, which is for my good. Grow me in the discipline of fixing my thoughts on You and what is true so that I can live in perfect peace. Amen.

*Day 20*

# CLOSE COMFORTER

> May the God of hope fill you with all joy and peace as you trust in him, so that you may overflow with hope by the power of the Holy Spirit.
>
> Romans 15:13

JOY AND SORROW can coexist because joy is wrapped up in the unchanging promise of who Jesus is and the fact that He never abandons His people. While He did not promise to eliminate difficulty when He left the earth in human form, He did promise to send a Comforter to help us through the hardship we will undoubtedly encounter.

Jesus kept His promise and sent His Spirit to dwell within us when we accept Him as Savior (John 14:16, 26). He gave us a close Comforter.

He is closer than your very breath. His goodness is running after you on your best day, your darkest day, and every kind of day in between. He is with you in the rejoicing on the mountaintop,

On the days you lack the *strength* to carry on, He will carry you and *sustain* you.

in your sorrow in the valley, and in the tension of the in-between. The tears you cry in secret are seen by Him. The fears you face and thoughts you wrestle that no one else is aware of—not even your closest earthly friend—are known by Him. I don't know all the answers to perfectly and practically navigate real hardships and suffering, but I know there is hope in the most unbearable things we face because of the One who walks with us, no matter how long or dark the night.

Live in the awareness of His goodness and nearness, and be led by the light of His truth. Your trust in Him will keep you moving forward. He is the source of joy and peace that never runs out. When we experience change, our thoughts and feelings shift, but our Comforter never does. He is constant and remains close. On the days you lack the strength to carry on, He will carry you and sustain you.

Remember that today, and in every moment, your Comforter is near, and He deeply cares for you.

> For his anger lasts only a moment,
> but his favor lasts a lifetime;
> weeping may stay for the night,
> but rejoicing comes in the morning.
> **Psalm 30:5**

**REFLECTION AND APPLICATION:** How have you experienced Jesus as the close Comforter? How does knowing that He is near help you to navigate the hardships you face? What fear, anxiety, or worry does the truth from today's devotional replace?

**PRAYER:** Jesus, thank You for sending the Comforter to lead me according to Your truth in every circumstance. Keep me continually aware of Your goodness, kindness, and nearness. Amen.

## *Day 21*

# SECURE

"Blessed [with spiritual security] is the man who believes
*and* trusts in *and* relies on the Lord
And whose hope *and* confident expectation is the Lord.
"For he will be [nourished] like a tree planted by the waters,
That spreads out its roots by the river;
And will not fear the heat when it comes;
But its leaves will be green *and* moist.
And it will not be anxious *and* concerned in a year of drought
Nor stop bearing fruit."

Jeremiah 17:7–8 AMP

I DEFINE *SECURE* two ways: (1) fixed or fastened so as to not give way, become loose, or be lost, and (2) feeling safe, stable, and free from fear or anxiety.

A few years ago, the Lord gave me the word *secure* to hold on to. I didn't understand it at the time, but I quickly realized that security was the opposite of the two things I was at war with internally—fear and insecurity.

I have learned the hard way that we will never find security in our knowledge of what comes next, but our trust in the One who created us, who goes before us, and who is always with us. When we feel unsettled, we can stand on the truth that our future is secure in Him. Our identity and value are secure in the truth that we have been created in the image of God and set apart for His glory and in His unconditional and unchanging love. Because of His love, we don't have to spend our lives striving for acceptance.

When things change, He will remain constant.

When people fail, He will be faithful.

When life is uncertain, His goodness is still sure.

Your steps are established. Your days are numbered. Even the very number of hairs on your head is known by God (see Luke 12:7). Your fears and failures don't disqualify you from the purpose He has prepared for you. When you submit to His authority, His plan for your life will prevail. Hold fast to this hope when you find yourself feeling anxious or insecure and when fearful thoughts creep in and whisper lies.

Run to Jesus and rest in Him. Freedom is found in the truth of His Word, and security is found in placing every detail of your life into His hands. When your heart and flesh mislead you, His Spirit will redirect you and His strength will sustain you . . . and His strength never runs out.

Your fears and failures don't disqualify you from the *purpose* He has *prepared* for you.

> My flesh and my heart may fail,
> but God is the strength of my heart
> and my portion forever.
> **Psalm 73:26**

**REFLECTION AND APPLICATION:** What have you attempted to find security in outside of Jesus? What is the difference between putting your trust in Jesus and putting it in other people or things? What fear, anxiety, or worry does the truth from today's devotional replace?

**PRAYER:** Jesus, thank You for the promise of security found in You. When my heart and flesh fail and mislead me, remind me to run to You. Amen.

## *Day 22*

# WHAT THE WILDERNESS REVEALS

> Remember how the Lord your God led you all the way in the wilderness these forty years, to humble and test you in order to know what was in your heart, whether or not you would keep his commands.
>
> Deuteronomy 8:2

SOMETHING I OFTEN take note of is the fact that many of the psalms were written from within the wilderness. It's a reminder of something that many of us have heard: God wastes nothing, not even the least desirable parts of our lives and our stories.

In Psalm 63 David writes,

> You, God, are my God,
> earnestly I seek you;

I thirst for you,
my whole being longs for you,
in a dry and parched land
where there is no water.

I have seen you in the sanctuary
and beheld your power and your glory.
Because your love is better than life,
my lips will glorify you.
I will praise you as long as I live,
and in your name I will lift up my hands.
I will be fully satisfied as with the richest of foods;
with singing lips my mouth will praise you.

On my bed I remember you;
I think of you through the watches of the night.
Because you are my help,
I sing in the shadow of your wings.
I cling to you;
your right hand upholds me.

Those who want to kill me will be destroyed;
they will go down to the depths of the earth.
They will be given over to the sword
and become food for jackals.

But the king will rejoice in God;
all who swear by God will glory in him,
while the mouths of liars will be silenced.

Such valuable lessons are revealed to us if we don't run from the tension of the challenges we experience.

In seasons of drought,
our souls thirst for *living* water
that is *only* found in Jesus.

The wilderness has a way of increasing our awareness of our need for Jesus. In the wilderness, our desperation for Jesus increases and, therefore, our dependence on Him grows. Hardship often draws us to seek Him earnestly. In physical lack, our spiritual eyes are often opened to see things more like He does. In seasons of drought, our souls thirst for living water that is only found in Jesus. When we feel pressed, we are more likely to give genuine praise that flows from our hearts.

In the wilderness, we cannot deny our need for the One whose hand upholds us. If you seek Him in the wilderness, you will experience one of the greatest gifts He can give—a deeper desire for Him and a greater understanding of who He is on the other side. Instead of attempting to run from the challenges you face, run to Him in the midst of them.

> I know what it is to be in need, and I know what it is to have plenty. I have learned the secret of being content in any and every situation, whether well fed or hungry, whether living in plenty or in want. I can do all this through him who gives me strength.
>
> **Philippians 4:12–13**

**REFLECTION AND APPLICATION:** Why do you think God allows us to walk through the wilderness? How can we learn from David's response to walking through the wilderness in Psalm 63? What fear, anxiety, or worry does the truth from today's devotional replace?

**PRAYER:** Jesus, give me eyes to see what You desire to reveal to me in every season. When I walk through the wilderness, increase my desperation for and dependence on You. Amen.

*Day 23*

# MAKING UP YOUR MIND

> Whether you turn to the right or to the left, your ears will hear a voice behind you, saying, "This is the way; walk in it."
>
> Isaiah 30:21

YOU AND I CAN either allow fear to dictate our decision-making and determine our future or we can put our confident trust in who God is and what His Word says. We will all look back on our lives either having trusted Him or wondering what would have happened if we did. I don't know about you, but I don't want to wonder; I want to experience nothing less than all of what He has for me.

Fear leads to confusion, compromise, and comparison when it comes to who God has called you to be and what He has called you to do.

His Word leads to clarity, steadfastness, and security when it comes to His plan for our lives.

Being led by truth does not mean you will know what is coming next but that your life is safe in the hands of the One who always does. When you are uncertain, move forward with confidence in His instruction and guidance. Keep your desire to honor Him before you and trust that He will be glorified in whatever you do.

We often complicate what He has made simple. If we're following Jesus, we should not live our lives in constant fear of making the wrong decision. Instead, following Him allows us to walk in the joy and freedom of surrendering with confidence, knowing that His plan and purpose for our lives will ultimately prevail. He will honor your desire to honor Him in the steps you take and decisions you make. Stay in step with the Spirit, knowing and applying His Word, and you will not be misled.

> You will decide on a matter, and it will be established
> for you,
> and light will shine on your ways.
>
> **Job 22:28 ESV**

Stay in *step* with the Spirit,
knowing and applying His Word,
and you will not be *misled*.

**REFLECTION AND APPLICATION:** What is the difference between being led by fear and being led by truth? If applicable, write down a decision you have to make and how you will be led by truth in the steps you take. What fear, anxiety, or worry does the truth from today's devotional replace?

**PRAYER:** Jesus, help me to keep the desire to honor You before me always. I know that when I follow Your lead, I will not be misled. Amen.

## Day 24

# CAST YOUR BURDEN

> Cast your burden on the Lord [release it] and He
> will sustain *and* uphold you;
> He will never allow the righteous to be shaken (slip,
> fall, fail).
>
> Psalm 55:22 AMP

READING THE AMPLIFIED BIBLE version of Psalm 55 recently led me to ask myself, *What burdens am I holding on to that He has invited me to release?*

I don't know about you, but I play the game of cast and carry far too often. It's not that I don't cast my cares on the Lord; it's the fact that I pick them back up just as quickly as I handed them over. It's a vicious and exhausting cycle.

The word *release* stood out to me from verse 22. To release means to stop carrying. It means to let go—and not to let go to later pick back up but to really, truly let go. Release means freedom, it means surrender, it means that it is no longer mine

to carry or try to control. I think that's often why I hold on so long, because even though my burdens are crushing, I like the control of having them in my own hands.

Isn't it amazing that God offers to carry the weight of our fears, concerns, failures, and the frustrations that consume us, yet so often we choose to remain consumed, hindered, and tired of being tired? I am so thankful that His Word is active and alive. We all need the reminder that the invitation to release our burdens to Jesus is open. He has not changed His mind about His willingness to carry the things we feel consumed and overwhelmed by.

He is gracious.

He is patient.

He is kind.

He longs to relieve you of the load you are carrying, whatever it may be, but first you have to let go of it once and for all. That is a choice you must make. In exchange, He promises to sustain you. This trade is far from fair, but He willingly takes it because He wants you to trust in and rely on Him.

So let me ask you this: Are you holding on to any burdens that God is inviting you to release?

Lay them down. Let them go. And this time, don't pick them back up. And don't pick up another load either. The burdens of this world are far better off in His capable hands.

> Cast all your anxiety on him because he cares for you.
> **1 Peter 5:7**

**REFLECTION AND APPLICATION:** What does it mean to cast your burdens on the Lord? What do you need to release into His hands? What fear, anxiety, or worry does the truth from today's devotional replace?

**PRAYER:** Jesus, thank You for caring for me. I release the burdens I am carrying into Your hands. Protect me from the temptation to pick them back up and hold on to control. Amen.

# *Day 25*

# EVEN IN THE STORM

Immediately after this, Jesus insisted that his disciples get back into the boat and cross to the other side of the lake, while he sent the people home. After sending them home, he went up into the hills by himself to pray. Night fell while he was there alone.

Meanwhile, the disciples were in trouble far away from land, for a strong wind had risen, and they were fighting heavy waves. About three o'clock in the morning Jesus came toward them, walking on the water. When the disciples saw him walking on the water, they were terrified. In their fear, they cried out, "It's a ghost!"

But Jesus spoke to them at once. "Don't be afraid," he said. "Take courage. I am here!"

Then Peter called to him, "Lord, if it's really you, tell me to come to you, walking on the water."

"Yes, come," Jesus said.

So Peter went over the side of the boat and walked on the water toward Jesus. But when he saw the strong wind and the waves, he was terrified and began to sink. "Save me, Lord!" he shouted.

Jesus immediately reached out and grabbed him. "You have so little faith," Jesus said. "Why did you doubt me?"

When they climbed back into the boat, the wind stopped. Then the disciples worshiped him. "You really are the Son of God!" they exclaimed.

Matthew 14:22–33 NLT

COULD WE BE WISHING away the very thing that God wants to use to reveal Himself to us in a greater way? The story of Jesus walking on the water in Matthew 14 is a notable example of this.

If it wasn't for the storm in this situation, the disciples would not have witnessed Jesus's power to both calm the storm and walk on water. Although they were fearful in the moment, the storm ultimately increased their confidence in who Jesus was. Fear led to doubt, but fixing their eyes on Jesus increased their faith.

You may have heard this story many times, but I pray it changes your perspective about the storms and struggles you are experiencing. Instead of wishing them away, invite Jesus to increase your faith in Him no matter what. Fixing your eyes on

Fear led to doubt, but *fixing* their eyes on Jesus *increased* their faith.

Him will challenge your doubt, increase your faith, and leave you to be more confident in His power—not just in the stories you hear but in your life personally.

What's even better than being removed from the storm? Having a greater revelation of who Jesus is amid the waves.

> When you pass through the waters, I will be with you;
> And through the rivers, they will not overwhelm you.
> When you walk through fire, you will not be scorched,
> Nor will the flame burn you.
>
> **Isaiah 43:2 AMP**

**REFLECTION AND APPLICATION:** How does this story in Matthew 14 change your outlook about being in the storm? What fear, anxiety, or worry does the truth from today's devotional replace?

**PRAYER:** Jesus, help me not to wish away the things You want to use to reveal Yourself to me. Give me faith to fix my eyes on You even in the storm. Amen.

*Day 26*

# THIS I KNOW

> The Lord makes firm the steps
> of the one who delights in him;
> though he may stumble, he will not fall,
> for the Lord upholds him with his hand.
>
> Psalm 37:23–24

BECAUSE OF MY HUMAN NATURE, I tend to be consumed by uncertainty. I often find myself in fearful spirals about the things that are out of my control. I have learned that what I do know about Jesus is more powerful than every uncertainty I encounter. Living confident of this reality allows me to live more certain of what I do know than uncertain and consumed by what I don't.

Here are some things I know:

I was not made to know everything.

I am not made to carry the weight of the unknown.

I don't have the full-picture view of my life.

**The fear of the unknown cannot *consume* you when you stand firm on the *promises* that are yours in and through Jesus.**

While we often think that knowing everything will solve our problems, we would be overwhelmed if we did. And if we knew everything, we would have no need to depend on Jesus. While our knowledge is limited, we have been given the opportunity to walk with the One who does and is in control of all things. Instead of spending our lives trying to figure out the answer to every unknown, we should spend them in pursuit of the One who nothing is unknown to.

He knows everything.

He carries our heavy, unbearable burdens.

He sees the full picture when all we see is right now.

He cannot be overwhelmed.

He cannot be defeated.

He cannot be anything less than good.

He is with us.

He is for us.

The future God has prepared for those who trust in Him is full of hope.

The fear of the unknown cannot consume you when you stand firm on the promises that are yours in and through Jesus. Victory is in Him.

> "For I know the plans I have for you," declares the Lord, "plans to prosper you and not to harm you, plans to give you hope and a future."
>
> **Jeremiah 29:11**

**REFLECTION AND APPLICATION:** Why do you think God doesn't allow us to know everything? How does confidence in Him help when you feel consumed by the unknown? What fear, anxiety, or worry does the truth from today's devotional replace?

**PRAYER:** Jesus, fill me with more trust in what I know about You than worry about what I am uncertain about. Increase my faith in the promise that Your plans are to give me hope and a future. Amen.

# *Day 27*

# REFUGE + STRENGTH

God is our refuge and strength,
an ever-present help in trouble.

Psalm 46:1

IN JESUS, you have not only a helper but an ever-present helper. To be ever-present means to always be there. Jesus is also all-knowing. In every circumstance, you have access to the One who knows exactly what to do because He has gone before you. He sees what is coming long before you do.

I understand what it's like to wrestle with wishing that God would just give you the answer when you ask, but it's also important to recognize that His ways are higher. Because of His love for us, He doesn't just give us what we want but what we really need. We want the short and effortless way, but He sees purpose in the longer, more challenging way that we cannot see. Instead of removing trouble or revealing the answer right away,

> He doesn't just give us
> what we *want*
> but what we really *need*.

He often leads us through a process that allows Him to reveal His character to us in an undeniable way.

We have a helper who continually teaches us to trust in and rely on Him. He doesn't just want us to know what His Word says about Him; He wants us to encounter who He is for ourselves. Everything changes when our faith becomes personal. The gift of experiencing trouble and trials is that they create an opportunity for our confidence in our helper to grow. I once heard it put this way: "An obstacle is an opportunity to have a moment with God." Obstacles allow Him to reveal Himself to us in a more undeniable way.

Jesus wants to reveal Himself not only as your helper but also as your refuge, your place of rest and safety, and your strength that sustains you through it all. When His help doesn't come in the way you hoped, consider what He may be wanting to teach you about who He is in the situation you are walking through.

Despite how things may seem, He is never distant, absent, or uninvolved. God is with you. He knows what you need. Trust Him as your ever-present help.

> So we can say with confidence,
>
> "The Lord is my helper,
> so I will have no fear.
> What can mere people do to me?"
>
> **Hebrews 13:6 NLT**

**REFLECTION AND APPLICATION:** How does this characteristic of God as refuge and strength help in overcoming fear? What does it mean to you personally to know that He is ever-present? What fear, anxiety, or worry does the truth from today's devotional replace?

**PRAYER:** Jesus, thank You for being my refuge, strength, and an ever-present help in trouble. Help me to see life's obstacles as an opportunity to experience Your goodness in an undeniable way. Amen.

*Day 28*

# SEEN TEARS, KNOWN FEARS

> Because of the LORD's great love we are not
> consumed,
> for his compassions never fail.
>
> Lamentations 3:22

NO FEAR YOU FACE or tear you cry is unknown by God. When it comes to your life, not a detail goes unnoticed by Him. I think it's important to start today with the fact that Jesus is not disappointed in or dismissive of the real challenges we face on this side of heaven. In fact, He understands because He willingly chose to walk the earth in human form so that He could sympathize with us in sorrow and suffering.

Scripture goes as far as saying that He both collects our tears in a bottle and delights in every detail of our lives (see Psalm 56:8). He knows, He understands, and He cares deeply about everything we go through. One of the things I love most about the character of Jesus seen throughout Scripture is that He gives people space to feel and then continually points them back to the hope they have in Him.

He is a compassionate and intentional Savior. He doesn't shy away from the reality of the hard and heavy circumstances we encounter or the fears we have, but He comes close and leads us in living a life of abundance and freedom. Knowing Him doesn't mean we will have a life that is absent of all fear and pain but a life of peace in the midst of fear and pain. A life of freedom from fear doesn't suggest we will never be afraid but that our trust in Him will help us to overcome and experience victory over our fears.

Our fears, flaws, and failures should send us running to, not away from, the One who sees our tears and knows our fears. It is through nearness to Him alone that we will experience fullness of life and freedom from fear.

> You keep track of all my sorrows.
> You have collected all my tears in your bottle.
> You have recorded each one in your book.
>
> **Psalm 56:8 NLT**

He knows, He understands,
and He cares *deeply*
about *everything* we go through.

**REFLECTION AND APPLICATION:** Why is it important to know that Jesus doesn't dismiss your feelings and fears? What is the significance of Jesus collecting your tears? What fear, anxiety, or worry does the truth from today's devotional replace?

**PRAYER:** Jesus, thank You for seeing my tears and knowing my fears. Remind me to run to You to find peace in pain and to experience victory over fear. Amen.

## *Day 29*

# PRESS ON

> I press on to reach the end of the race and receive the heavenly prize for which God, through Christ Jesus, is calling us.
>
> Philippians 3:14 NLT

THERE WILL BE TIMES when you ask God for a clear direction or the next assignment to move forward, and His answer will be as simple as, "Stay the course." While it will be frustrating and even confusing in the moment, one day you will recognize His purpose and intentionality in that response. How do I know? Through following Him.

I used to think the most important thing was where I was headed, but now I know that growing in my confidence and relationship with Jesus on the journey is far more important. He doesn't want you to place your confidence in where you are going but in His guidance along the way. He is developing in you dependence on Him with every step you take.

I am convinced that if Jesus were a GPS, His instructions would sound something like this:

keep moving forward
take a slight left
turn around here—or there
stop here for a moment and rest with Me

The key is that, with Jesus, we often get those directions as they come and less frequently as we are miles away from Him. His guidance conflicts with our tendency to hurry, hustle, and always want to know where we are going and how we are getting there. He leads us each along a unique and intentional path to knowing and trusting Him and learning to keep our eyes fixed on His face. If He revealed what was next too soon, we would miss what He is teaching us about His character and what He is maturing in our faith. His process keeps us present in the now and prepares us for what He is calling us to next.

He promises us His unfailing guidance. If you are following Him, you will never be misled, not even when you find yourself in the wilderness. Stay the course. Keep running the race of faith set before you. Stay consistent in stewarding what is in front of you as He prepares you for whatever is next. He won't lead you where He hasn't gone before.

He won't *lead* you where
He hasn't *gone* before.

> But as for you, be strong and do not give up, for your work will be rewarded.
>
> **2 Chronicles 15:7**

**REFLECTION AND APPLICATION:** How does the way Jesus leads contradict your desire for comfort? What does His process produce in you? What fear, anxiety, or worry does the truth from today's devotional replace?

**PRAYER:** Jesus, grow my confidence in Your unfailing guidance and strengthen me to endure in following You. Thank You that You don't lead me where You don't go with me. Amen.

# *Day 30*

# REMAIN

> Remain in Me, and I [will remain] in you. Just as no branch can bear fruit by itself without remaining in the vine, neither can you [bear fruit, producing evidence of your faith] unless you remain in Me.
>
> John 15:4 AMP

REMAIN:

- to stay in the place that one has been occupying
- to abide or dwell (not a onetime occurrence, but something that is ongoing)

I ONCE HEARD that all you have to do to drift is nothing. Those simple words have caused me to approach my relationship with Jesus with greater intentionality than ever before. It's easy to grow complacent and weary when it comes to walking with Him, especially when we choose our comfort over His instruction. This is why God calls us to remain in Him.

Healthy growth in our faith requires that we stay connected to the source that is providing us with life. It is the only way to live the abundant life available to us. Stay diligent in drawing

When you find yourself becoming *complacent* and experiencing weariness, stay *steadfast* in seeking and surrendering to Him.

near to Jesus. Stay confident and hopeful in His plan. When you find yourself becoming complacent and experiencing weariness, stay steadfast in seeking and surrendering to Him. Be intentional in growing in the knowledge and application of His Word to your life.

Remember that apart from your source, Jesus, you can do nothing worthwhile, and there is nothing more valuable to pursue than your relationship with Him. Set Him and your desire to honor Him continually before you, and make Him the treasure of your life. Remember where He has brought you from and keep moving forward into all that He has prepared for you. Live recognizably set apart.

Not just life but abundant life is found in Him alone. Remaining in and following Him won't always be easy, but they produce only good things.

> But the fruit of the Spirit is love, joy, peace, patience, kindness, goodness, faithfulness, gentleness, self-control; against such things there is no law.
>
> **Galatians 5:22–23 ESV**

**REFLECTION AND APPLICATION:** What is the importance of continually remaining in Jesus? How does remaining help to overcome fear? What fear, anxiety, or worry does the truth from today's devotional replace?

**PRAYER:** Jesus, thank You for the greatest gift of relationship with You. Guide me in living a life of intentionally remaining connected to You so that I can experience the abundance of nearness to You. Amen.

*Day 31*

# HIS WORD, YOUR WEAPON

Finally, be strong in the Lord and in the strength of his might. Put on the whole armor of God, that you may be able to stand against the schemes of the devil. For we do not wrestle against flesh and blood, but against the rulers, against the authorities, against the cosmic powers over this present darkness, against the spiritual forces of evil in the heavenly places. Therefore take up the whole armor of God, that you may be able to withstand in the evil day, and having done all, to stand firm. Stand therefore, having fastened on the belt of truth, and having put on the breastplate of righteousness, and, as shoes for your feet, having put on the readiness given by the gospel of peace. In all circumstances take up the shield of faith, with which you can extinguish all the flaming darts of the evil one; and take the helmet of salvation, and the sword of the Spirit, which is the word of God.

Ephesians 6:10–17 ESV

IT WAS RECENTLY pointed out to me that the armor of God includes only one weapon—God's Word—because the Bible is all we need to be victorious in the spiritual battles we face, especially the battle of the mind. The rest of the armor of God is for our protection.

The thing about a weapon, though, is that to win a battle, the weapon must be used. The weapon of the Word must be used in our lives to protect us from the schemes of the enemy. Satan knows that one of the best ways to weaken us is to attack our minds, so he spends much of his time whispering lies in attempts to confuse, distract, and discourage us from God's plan for our lives.

Living in awareness of what God's Word says is not enough to experience victory over these lies. We must know His Word, apply it, and establish it as the guide and standard according to which we live. The Bible must take authority over feelings, opinions, and experiences.

The enemy's tactics are strategic. He will do anything to keep you from experiencing the life of peace and abundance you have access to through Jesus. But his strategies cannot prevail against the weapon of the sword of the Spirit, which is active and alive

Even in moments where you feel *defeated*, you will not be destroyed. You have been given the *greatest* weapon.

in us. Every instruction it provides is purposeful, intentional, and for our good.

Know God's Word, declare it over and apply it to your life, and you will walk in victory. Even in moments where you feel defeated, you will not be destroyed. You have been given the greatest weapon.

> Every word of God proves true;
> he is a shield to those who take refuge in him.
> **Proverbs 30:5 ESV**

**REFLECTION AND APPLICATION:** What is a lie that the enemy has recently whispered to you? How does the weapon of God's Word battle against that lie? What fear, anxiety, or worry does the truth from today's devotional replace?

**PRAYER:** Jesus, thank You for providing Your Word as a weapon. Guide me in knowing and applying it to experience victory over the enemy's attempts to discourage, distract, and defeat me from Your plan and purpose for my life. Amen.

*Day 32*

# WITHOUT FEAR OF THE FUTURE

> She is clothed with strength and dignity,
> and she laughs without fear of the future.
> Proverbs 31:25 NLT

I INTENTIONALLY included this Scripture because, while it is one of the most quoted, it is one of the most challenging verses to live out. These words have become ones that we memorize and quote quickly, but if we are honest, the directive to stay strong in the face of uncertainty in Proverbs 31:25 seems unattainable when we are faced with overwhelming fears and unknowns. God's heart is not for His people to just know these words but for us to arrive at a place where our confidence in who He is consumes our fear of what is to come. It is possible, but only through taking Him at His Word.

We can only laugh without fear of the future and live full of expectation for the days ahead when we wholeheartedly trust the One who holds our future in His hands. Having faith that Jesus

> *Laughing* without fear of the future is a result of confidence in the One who *never* changes.

is ultimately in control allows us to release the fear of what is unknown and out of our control. Trusting Jesus does not mean that we won't be presented with valid reasons to be afraid; it means that we can live in the freedom that is a result of holding fast to His faithfulness. Because of who Jesus is and what His Word promises, we should be living more expectant, hopeful, and confident than we are dreading, discouraged, and anxious. Instead of dragging our feet, we can walk with our heads held high.

We may not always know what is coming next, but we can rest assured that He is always good. When we really believe that He is all that we need, we can rejoice no matter what comes. Laughing without fear of the future is a result of confidence in the One who never changes. Unspeakable joy is found in Him alone, even in the face of our greatest fears and defeats.

> Therefore do not worry about tomorrow, for tomorrow will worry about itself. Each day has enough trouble of its own.
>
> **Matthew 6:34**

**REFLECTION AND APPLICATION:** How should trusting Jesus change your perspective of the future? Where might He be calling you to rejoice where you currently feel discouraged or defeated? What fear, anxiety, or worry does the truth from today's devotional replace?

**PRAYER:** Jesus, I want my confidence in who You are to consume my fears about the unknown. Help me to wholeheartedly trust You with my future like the woman described in Proverbs 31:25, because I know this is Your desire for me. Amen.

*Day 33*

# DRAW NEAR

But for me it is good to be near God;
I have made the Lord God my refuge,
that I may tell of all your works.

Psalm 73:28 ESV

TO BE *CLOSE* is to be in a position so as to be very near to someone or something, with very little space between.

The life you live will reveal your proximity to Jesus. Your nearness to or distance from Him is on display whether you recognize it or not. The closer you are to Him, the more like your Maker you will become and the more your thoughts, words, and actions will reflect Him to the world around you. Don't just claim to know Jesus or know about Him, really know Him. Get in His Scriptures and spend more time at His feet than you spend anywhere else.

He knows everything about you—every thought you think, every fear you face, and every desire you have—yet He longs to hear directly from you because His greatest desire is relationship with you. How do I know? Because He died to restore that relationship where sin once separated us from the ability

The *closer* you draw to your Maker, the *clearer* you will reflect Him.

to draw near to Him. Continually and intentionally draw near to Him and listen long enough to hear His heart for you so you can be reminded of His plans for your life.

As you draw close to Him, He will draw close to you. He is a personal Savior, father, and friend. He will lead you into a deeper understanding of who He is and what His Word says and means for you personally. As a result, your faith will increase, your hope will increase, your confidence (in who He is and who He has called you to be) will increase, your joy will increase, and your peace will increase, despite the circumstances around you.

As you draw near, the cares of the world will grow more distant. Your discipline to know and to love Him more will become your delight. You will be continually purified and transformed to reflect His image. The closer you draw to your Maker, the clearer you will reflect Him. His heart is for you to live a life of nearness to Him.

> Come close to God [with a contrite heart] and He will come close to you. Wash your hands, you sinners; and purify your [unfaithful] hearts, you double-minded [people].
>
> **James 4:8 AMP**

**REFLECTION AND APPLICATION:** What are some examples of the evidence of a life of nearness to Jesus? How does it make you feel to know that He wants to hear from you personally even though He already knows every detail of your life? What fear, anxiety, or worry does the truth from today's devotional replace?

**PRAYER:** Jesus, I pray that my life is a reflection of my nearness to You. Thanks for drawing near to me as I draw near to You. Amen.

## *Day 34*

# PEACE

> For he himself is our peace, who has made the two groups one and has destroyed the barrier, the dividing wall of hostility, by setting aside in his flesh the law with its commands and regulations. His purpose was to create in himself one new humanity out of the two, thus making peace, and in one body to reconcile both of them to God through the cross, by which he put to death their hostility.
>
> Ephesians 2:14–16

JESUS DOES NOT just give us peace; He is our peace.

When we walk with Him, we can have peace regardless of what is going on in our lives or in the world around us. This is one of the reasons John 15:5 calls us to abide (or remain) in Him when it says, "I am the vine; you are the branches. If you remain in me and I in you, you will bear much fruit; apart from me you can do nothing." That last part reminds us that we cannot have peace outside of nearness to Jesus. We can't have the abundant life He intends for His children while we're burdened by fear. Remaining in Him is remaining in peace.

**Peace does not mean the *absence* of pain or chaos but the promise of His *presence* in the midst of it.**

Peace is not a fleeting feeling (although it does affect our feelings); it is the result of dwelling. It's not something you can try harder to earn; it is a product of surrender. Peace is achieved when you recognize that you can't carry the weight of life on your own and live in awareness that He is with you through it all. Peace does not mean the absence of pain or chaos but the promise of His presence in the midst of it.

Jesus does not withhold Himself from us, so peace is always accessible to us. Stop searching for peace outside of Jesus. Stop attempting to earn it. Instead, surrender to His sovereignty. Remember that what is out of your control rests in the hands of the One who is in control of all things.

When your thoughts wage war against you, peace is your portion and promise in Him.

> Great peace have those who love your law,
> and nothing can make them stumble.
> **Psalm 119:165**

**REFLECTION AND APPLICATION:** Where do you currently lack peace? Where have you attempted to find peace outside of Jesus? What fear, anxiety, or worry does the truth from today's devotional replace?

**PRAYER:** Jesus, You are my peace regardless of how I feel or how my circumstances may seem. Lead me to dwell in Your presence daily. Amen.

*Day 35*

# POWER, LOVE, AND A SOUND MIND

For God has not given us a spirit of fear, but of power and of love and of a sound mind.

2 Timothy 1:7 NKJV

For God gave us a spirit not of fear but of power and love and self-control.

2 Timothy 1:7 ESV

I **INTENTIONALLY** included both translations of this verse because the comparison stood out to me. It led me to these two conclusions.

First, a spirit of fear is not from God. It can be difficult to understand why God allows us to experience fear or other challenges in life. In Genesis, we see that when God created the earth, His design was perfect and without flaw. It did not include pain,

*Remember* that you have not been given a spirit of fear, but a spirit of *power*, *love*, and a *sound mind* because of Jesus.

sorrow, suffering, fear, anxiety, or even death. These are all results of sin that He never intended for us to experience.

While we can't change the fact that we live in a world suffering from the consequences of sin, we can choose to walk in the help, guidance, and comfort God provides. Doing so allows us to have the peace that He provides when we are afraid. Remember that you have not been given a spirit of fear, but a spirit of power, love, and a sound mind because of Jesus.

Second, a sound mind doesn't just happen. A sound mind is a result of a heart and mind continually fixed on the promises, faithfulness, and goodness of God. Having a sound mind does not happen by coincidence but requires intentionality, discipline, and obedience. This is why "a sound mind" and "self-control" are interchangeable in 2 Timothy 1:7, because a sound mind requires self-control. Having peace requires not just knowing the truth of God's Word but applying it and allowing it to guide, instruct, and correct you as you navigate living in the world—but not of it.

Remember today that you have not been given a spirit of fear but a spirit of power, love, and a sound mind through Christ alone.

> My prayer is not that you take them out of the world but that you protect them from the evil one. They are not of the world, even as I am not of it. Sanctify them by the truth; your word is truth.
>
> **John 17:15–17**

**REFLECTION AND APPLICATION:** How does having a sound mind require self-control? How does Scripture instruct us to navigate living in the world but not of it? What fear, anxiety, or worry does the truth from today's devotional replace?

**PRAYER:** Jesus, I recognize that fear does not come from You. Help me to practice self-control, which allows me to walk in the power and love, and with the sound mind, You have given me. Amen.

*Day 36*

# DECEIVED BY DISCOURAGEMENT

Why, my soul, are you downcast?
  Why so disturbed within me?
Put your hope in God,
  for I will yet praise him,
  my Savior and my God.

Psalm 43:5

DISCOURAGEMENT can be like a fog that distorts our view of what is going on around us or even right in front of us. I was recently talking with a friend about a discouraging situation I have been facing. I was honestly having a bit of a "woe is me" moment.

She loved me enough to say a hard thing. "Maddie, I think the enemy is trying to deceive you with this discouragement you are experiencing. From the outside I can see how God is working in your life and using this to deepen your trust in Him. Disappointment won't last forever."

You see, the enemy wants to use discouragement to deceive us into believing that we are stuck, that God isn't working, and that we should throw in the towel. He wants the fog of discouragement to detach us from our awareness of Jesus's nearness and the way Jesus is working beyond what we can currently see.

The thing about fog, though, is that it always lifts—or we move past it. There is always something on the other side of what we cannot see. In contrast, Jesus uses our discouragement to develop, deepen, and increase our trust in who He is and the way He works. There are just some things that can't be learned on the mountaintop like they can be in, let's call it, the valley of the fog of discouragement. No, I don't think that Jesus wants us to be discouraged, but we also live in a sin-saturated world that keeps us from living the perfect life that He originally intended.

Because brokenness and pain are unavoidable in a sinful world, He redeems the painful experiences we encounter for our good and for His glory. If you are walking through discouragement today, don't allow the enemy to deceive you into believing that this will last forever or that Jesus isn't working beyond your circumstances. There is more to the story.

You are not stuck. He will either lead you out or He will be faithful to lead you through. In the meantime, if you will turn to

*Jesus* uses our discouragement to develop, deepen, and increase our *trust* in who He is and the way He works.

and trust in Jesus, He will produce purpose from the pain of this season. He will redeem your discouragement by deepening your dependence on Him and increasing your strength.

> But those who hope in the Lord
> will renew their strength.
> They will soar on wings like eagles;
> they will run and not grow weary,
> they will walk and not be faint.
> **Isaiah 40:31**

**REFLECTION AND APPLICATION:** How has Jesus used discouragement in your life to deepen your dependence on Him? How do you feel knowing that He is working beyond what you can currently see? What fear, anxiety, or worry does the truth from today's devotional replace?

**PRAYER:** Jesus, use discouragement in my life to increase my dependence on You. You are always near and are constantly working beyond my understanding. Renew my strength today. Amen.

# *Day 37*

# TAKE HEART

> I have told you these things, so that in me you may have peace. In this world you will have trouble. But take heart! I have overcome the world.
>
> John 16:33

**IT CAN BE CHALLENGING** to understand how a good Father whose plans for us are good not only says we might encounter trouble but guarantees that we will. When giving this guarantee, He also provides this instruction: "Take heart! I have overcome the world." This is one of my favorite things about Jesus—He doesn't shy away from hard things but also never leaves us without hope to hold on to.

To take heart means "to gain courage or confidence" or "to begin to feel hopeful."

In order to see Jesus's kindness through trials, we must view our circumstance through a different lens. We must look through spiritual eyes past the present moment of discomfort and recognize the opportunity being presented to us. We also must consider what He might be trying to produce within us through

**When we put our hope in *Him*, our *hope* will never fail.**

the things we wish He would remove us from. You don't have to like the trial, but you may have to endure it since there will be times when you can't change it. When you find yourself in that place, you have a choice to make.

You can either dwell in discouragement or receive Jesus's invitation to take heart and trust Him. When you choose the latter, your courage and confidence will increase. You will see that there is hope to be found even in what appears hopeless because He holds all things together. As much as we may desire a world without trouble, we have a greater promise to hold on to, a promise that He has overcome the world.

When we put our hope in Him, our hope will never fail.

> Be strong and take heart,
> all you who hope in the Lord.
> **Psalm 31:24**

> Consider it pure joy, my brothers and sisters, whenever you face trials of many kinds, because you know that the testing of your faith produces perseverance. Let perseverance finish its work so that you may be mature and complete, not lacking anything.
> **James 1:2–4**

**REFLECTION AND APPLICATION:** Where have you dwelled in discouragement where Jesus is inviting you to take heart? How can you consider trials joy when you walk with Him? What fear, anxiety, or worry does the truth from today's devotional replace?

**PRAYER:** Jesus, I take heart in the midst of trials and trouble because You have overcome the world. Help me to walk in the peace You provide. Amen.

# *Day 38*

# PROVIDER

> By his divine power, God has given us everything we need for living a godly life. We have received all of this by coming to know him, the one who called us to himself by means of his marvelous glory and excellence.
>
> 2 Peter 1:3 NLT

JESUS IS YOUR PROVIDER.

While that doesn't mean that you will get everything you want when you want it and in the package you expect it to arrive in, it does mean that He will not leave you without what you need for the fulfillment of His plan for your life.

We live in a culture that associates God's provision with an earthly idea of success that will satisfy a desire for materialistic things. The church falls into this mindset as well. The problem with this perspective is that it places an expectation on our Provider to deliver what He never promised. This leads many people to discouragement, disappointment, frustration, and feeling as though He has failed them.

His *provision* will sometimes look different than you hoped or prayed, but it does not change His perfect track record of *faithfulness*.

The truth is that His provision will sometimes look different than you hoped or prayed, but it does not change His perfect track record of faithfulness. Yes, He provides tangible treasures, but there is so much more. He ultimately provides in such a way that keeps us dependent on Him and helps us to recognize that in Him alone we have all that we need.

You will never be fully satisfied unless or until you recognize Jesus as both your greatest need AND desire. More than He longs for you to live a life of fleeting earthly prosperity, He longs for you to live a life of lasting eternal value. Instead of seeking provision, seek the Provider Himself. Open your eyes to what He may be trying to produce in you that is far more valuable than what you currently want.

Instead of relying on your own strength and strategy, surrender your wants, needs, dreams, and desires to Him. Submit your life to the authority of His plan and process, and you will live in His peace. His Word says that those who seek first the kingdom will not be left wanting.

Grab hold of this promise today.

> Seek the Kingdom of God above all else, and live righteously, and he will give you everything you need.
>
> **Matthew 6:33 NLT**

**REFLECTION AND APPLICATION:** What have you learned or been reminded of about God the Provider from reading today's devotion? How is His idea of provision different than yours? What fear, anxiety, or worry does the truth from today's devotional replace?

**PRAYER:** Jesus, thank You for being a perfect provider. I surrender my wants, dreams, needs, and desires to You and trust that You will be faithful. Amen.

## *Day 39*

# CREATED + CALLED

> For we are his workmanship, created in Christ Jesus for good works, which God prepared beforehand, that we should walk in them.
>
> Ephesians 2:10 ESV

I KNOW WHAT IT feels like to be called to something and to be met with feelings of fear, doubt, or uncertainty as you attempt to step into that calling. I know what it's like to question if God has selected the right person for what He is asking you to do. I know what it's like to try to talk yourself (and Him) out of what He has stirred your heart to do because it requires uncomfortable steps of obedience that feel too big for you in your own ability. I recently had this thought as I was wrestling through some of those fears, doubts, and uncertainties when it came to taking a step I felt called to take—"My Caller is also my Creator."

Don't wait to take the *step* until you aren't afraid. Feel the fear and move *forward* anyway.

That simple truth did not eliminate my insecurity, but it increased my confidence in the fact that He knows me better than I know myself or anyone else knows me. He knows where I have been, where I am, and where I am going, and He orders my steps and orchestrates my life accordingly and intentionally.

I don't know what God has called you to do or what steps He has called you to take, but I do know that this truth is the same for you. Your Caller is also your Creator.

When you are faced with feelings of insecurity and self-doubt, He doesn't change His mind about your calling. Instead of trying to find a way out, invite Him to increase your confidence in His strength, power, and ability to do through you what you feel unqualified to do.

Your Caller and Creator knows where you are going, how to get you there, and what you need for the journey. Don't wait to take the step until you aren't afraid. Feel the fear and move forward anyway. As you do, He will come alongside you.

> "Before I formed you in the womb I knew you,
> before you were born I set you apart;
> I appointed you as a prophet to the nations."
> "Alas, Sovereign Lord," I said, "I do not know how to speak; I am too young."
> . . . "Do not be afraid of them, for I am with you and will rescue you," declares the Lord.
>
> **Jeremiah 1:5–8**

**REFLECTION AND APPLICATION:** What do you feel called to that fear has hindered you from pursuing? What is the significance of Jesus being the One who both creates and calls His children? What fear, anxiety, or worry does the truth from today's devotional replace?

**PRAYER:** Jesus, I put my confidence in the fact that You have both created and called me. In the face of fear, doubt, and insecurity, guide me in surrendering to You. Amen.

## *Day 40*

# OVERWHELMED BY ANXIETY

For the Lord is good and his love endures forever;
his faithfulness continues through all
generations.

Psalm 100:5

BREATHE IN. BREATHE OUT. Each breath you take is a testimony of God's miraculous hand at work in your life. It's not as simple as it seems. There are a million little things working together at this moment for you to even be able to read these words. I share this to remind you that He is in control of even the littlest details we fail to consider at times.

Let your concerns be drowned out by your confidence that He can be nothing short of good. Ask that He will make you aware of His kindness and that He will bring His faithfulness to the forefront of your mind. Look at the Word, look at your life, look at the lives of those around you. Repeatedly, He has done exactly

> Let your concerns be drowned out by your *confidence* that He can be nothing short of *good*.

what He said He would do and continues to keep His promises; therefore, we have nothing to fear when we put our trust in Him.

Let what you do know have more authority in your life than what you don't know. Instead of being consumed by your concerns, live confident in the One who never fails.

Be careful not to be ruled by your thoughts and feelings. Let what you know about God's character reign over the things you are unsure of about life and what is to come.

The unknown can be overwhelming, but every detail of your life is seen and known by Him. There are no accidents or coincidences when it comes to the way God works, even when we don't understand what He is doing now.

Remember:

Whatever changes, He won't.

Whatever fails, He won't.

Whatever uncertainty you face, you can remain confident in who He is.

Yesterday, He was good. Today, He is good. Tomorrow and all the days to come, He will be good.

Whatever is coming must yield to His authority. Proclaim this promise over every anxious thought. Allow your trust in His faithfulness to consume your fears.

> If we are faithless,
> he remains faithful,
> for he cannot disown himself.
> **2 Timothy 2:13**

**REFLECTION AND APPLICATION:** Where have you allowed the unknown to consume you? How does confidence in who Jesus is ease anxiety toward the unknown? What fear, anxiety, or worry does the truth from today's devotional replace?

**PRAYER:** Jesus, let the promise of Your faithfulness consume my anxious thoughts. Thank You for never changing and never failing. You can be nothing short of good. Amen.

## Day 41

# A PRAYER FOR TODAY

> This is the confidence we have in approaching God: that if we ask anything according to his will, he hears us.
>
> 1 John 5:14

EVERYTHING THAT SCRIPTURE instructs is intentional and purposeful. One of those instructions is to pray continually, inviting Jesus into every area of our lives (see 1 Thess. 5:17). I find it amazing that nothing about our lives is unknown to God, but He cares so much about having a relationship with us that He wants to hear from us personally and consistently. Don't overcomplicate the purpose of prayer, and don't underestimate the power of communication with Jesus. Live a life of obedience to this instruction.

Here is a simple prayer copied directly from my journal. I would love you to join me in praying this today:

*Examine the posture of my heart daily, Lord. Is it pleasing to You?*

*Refine me in the areas and attitudes that don't reflect You. Help me to walk in joy, humility, truth, servanthood, and in awe and wonder of who You are. Let the thoughts in my mind, words in my mouth, and steps that I take be pleasing to You. I will not approach the days of my life with dread but with excitement and anticipation to be alive, to be Yours, and to be used by You!*

*I will operate in gladness. I will do whatever I have the privilege of doing for Your glory. You are the light of my days. You have my attention, my priority, and my yes. I don't overlook the miracle it is to be alive in this moment. I want to steward the miracle well and to the FULLEST. I do this by hearing, knowing, trusting, and doing what Your Word instructs. I don't want to be just a witness of what You are doing. I want to be a partaker, a participator! I want to join You, walk with You, talk with You, and abide in You.*

*Amen.*

When you can't find the words to pray, turn to His Word as a guide. Praying Scripture will never fail you. Jesus is our greatest example of going to the Father in prayer. Talk to Him daily. Thank Him for every good thing that comes from Him. Remind your heart of what He has spoken, and speak His promises over your circumstances. No matter what comes and goes, He remains, and He longs to hear from you. Approach Him with confidence that He will not only listen but respond.

## When you can't find the *words* to pray, turn to *His Word* as a guide.

> This, then, is how you should pray:
>
> "'Our Father in heaven,
> hallowed be your name,
> your kingdom come,
> your will be done,
>     on earth as it is in heaven.
> Give us today our daily bread.
> And forgive us our debts,
>     as we also have forgiven our debtors.
> And lead us not into temptation,
>     but deliver us from the evil one.'"
>
> **Matthew 6:9–13**

**REFLECTION AND APPLICATION:** Why does Jesus call you to pray continually? What are you currently anticipating with excitement for God to do in your life? What fear, anxiety, or worry does the truth from today's devotional replace?

**PRAYER:** Jesus, thank You that I can approach You with confidence. Help me to prioritize prayer in my everyday life. Amen.

## *Day 42*

# ADVOCATE

> My dear children, I write this to you so that you will not sin. But if anybody does sin, we have an advocate with the Father—Jesus Christ, the Righteous One. He is the atoning sacrifice for our sins, and not only for ours but also for the sins of the whole world.
>
> 1 John 2:1–2

HAVE YOU EVER FOUND yourself unsure of where to go, what to do, or what to even pray in a situation? If so, I have good news for you.

In John 16:7, Jesus says, "But very truly I tell you, it is for your good that I am going away. Unless I go away, the Advocate will not come to you; but if I go, I will send him to you."

I will never get over the fact that when Jesus ascended to heaven, He said it would be better if He weren't physically present with His people anymore. I can't imagine how the disciples—those who walked with Him and talked with Him and felt the nail scars in His hands—felt trying to understand how Jesus's physical absence could possibly be better than having Him by their side. In some ways, it must have felt as if they were being abandoned—but He had a plan. He was sending a promise, a gift, one that is still available to us today.

Jesus was sending an advocate—an intercessor, counselor, and helper. He was sending His present presence. He was sending His Spirit, whose purpose was and still is to point us to Jesus and to lead us along the path of His perfect plan. The Holy Spirit is our advocate and intercessor. An advocate is someone who pleads on another's behalf, and an intercessor is someone who intervenes on behalf of another, especially through prayer. Therefore, you do not have to fear or feel discouraged when you find yourself at a loss for words. You are not lost when you don't know where to go or what to do. You have not been left to wonder or wander. The One who knows the answers is guiding you and continually going to the Father on your behalf.

Isn't it beautiful to think that He is praying over you?

Though He may feel far, He is closer than your very breath.

Nothing is unknown to God or outside of His reach. He brings confidence and clarity to our uncertainties, and He will never leave us or forsake us.

The One who knows the answers is *guiding* you and continually going to the Father on *your* behalf.

> In the same way, the Spirit helps us in our weakness. We do not know what we ought to pray for, but the Spirit himself intercedes for us through wordless groans.
>
> **Romans 8:26**

**REFLECTION AND APPLICATION:** Why was it better for Jesus to be physically absent from earth? Why do we need the advocate (His Spirit)? What fear, anxiety, or worry does the truth from today's devotional replace?

**PRAYER:** Jesus, thank You for providing an advocate in Your Spirit. When I don't have the words to say, I trust that You know what I need and will intervene on my behalf. Amen.

# Day 43

# PROTECTOR

> What, then, shall we say in response to these things? If God is for us, who can be against us?
>
> Romans 8:31

JESUS IS OUR protector and defender. Not only is He our place to run to and rest in, but while we rest, He is working on our behalf. This promise includes, but is not limited to, physical protection. He is also a guard over our hearts and minds. He sees what is coming long before it arrives, and He guides us accordingly.

His instruction is for our protection. Live according to it.

His plans are for our good and never for our harm or destruction. Walk in His ways.

Keep these promises continually before you. At times, it may feel as though you are being tried beyond what you can bear. Remember that it is not in God's nature to allow you to be consumed. On the other hand, He is protecting you from things that you are entirely unaware of throughout your life. Nothing escapes Him.

> Our lack of ability to *recognize* Him never changes the fact that He is *there*.

Your protector cares.

Your protector hears.

Your protector delivers.

Stay in His presence. Yield to His process. His timing is perfect. Trust what He says when you can't trace His hand, and continue to call on Him. Sometimes His deliverance is undeniable. Other times it takes looking back to recognize the ways He was there all along. Our lack of ability to recognize Him never changes the fact that He is there.

You have a protector and defender who defeated death itself. When you put your trust in Him, you truly have nothing to fear. You may feel defeated, but you won't be destroyed. Since He is for you, nothing can prevail against you.

> The Lord is my rock, my fortress, and my savior;
> my God is my rock, in whom I find protection.
> He is my shield, the power that saves me,
> and my place of safety.
> He is my refuge, my savior,
> the one who saves me from violence.
> I called on the Lord, who is worthy of praise,
> and he saved me from my enemies.
>
> **2 Samuel 22:2–4 NLT**

**REFLECTION AND APPLICATION:** Where have you struggled to trust Jesus as your protector? Identify a time when it felt like He wasn't there, but looking back now, you can see how He was protecting you. What fear, anxiety, or worry does the truth from today's devotional replace?

**PRAYER:** Jesus, thank You for being my protector. Since You are for me, I know that nothing can prevail against me. Guide me in walking according to Your instruction, which is always for my good. Amen.

## *Day 44*

# TRUSTWORTHY

> God is faithful [He is reliable, trustworthy and ever true to His promise—He can be depended on], and through Him you were called into fellowship with His Son, Jesus Christ our Lord.
>
> 1 Corinthians 1:9 AMP

THE GOD WHO establishes the rhythm of the waves and sets the boundaries for the land and sea, the God who made the sky blue, tells the sun when to set, and sends the rain . . . the One who knows the number of grains of sand on the ground in all the earth and still takes note of the number of hairs on your head, that God is ordering your steps.

Who are you not to trust Him?

His thoughts are higher and His ways greater than you can even begin to imagine. Don't lose your wonder and awareness of the One who holds the world and your world in the palm of His hand. Since He can't fail, you have nothing to fear.

Thank Him.

Praise Him.

Hope and trust in Him.

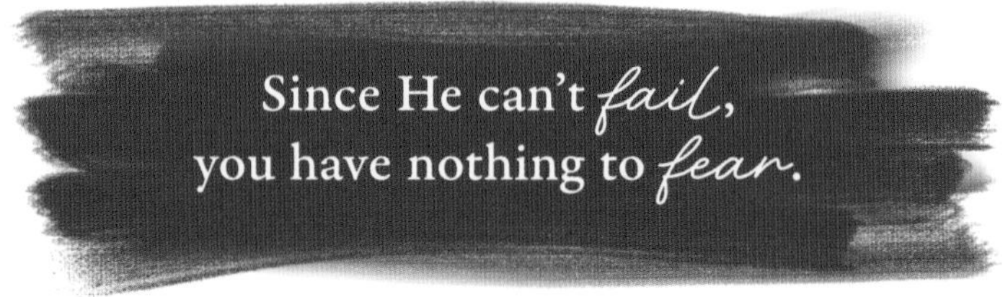


He knows the answers to all your questions. He is in control of what you are concerned about. He is not disappointed in your doubt but wants you to draw close to Him so that He can reveal Himself to you. His presence is everywhere. He is always working in both ways you can and cannot see. Nothing is impossible for Him or outside of His reach. In Him, you have all that you need.

Desire to be where He wants you to be, even when you don't understand why He has you there. Choose obedience even when it's uncomfortable. Trust Him even when you can't identify what He is doing because He has proven Himself trustworthy.

I can't tell you what the outcome of trusting Him will be, but I can assure you that it will be worth it. You may be small, but you are not insignificant to God. His plans for you are good.

He is worthy of your wholehearted trust.

> Listen to me, O family of Jacob,
>     Israel my chosen one!
> I alone am God,
>     the First and the Last.
> It was my hand that laid the foundations of the earth,
>     my right hand that spread out the heavens above.
> When I call out the stars,
>     they all appear in order.
>
> **Isaiah 48:12–13 NLT**

**REFLECTION AND APPLICATION:** How do these truths about who God is increase your trust in His ability to guide you? What fear, anxiety, or worry does the truth from today's devotional replace?

**PRAYER:** Jesus, You are unfailingly trustworthy and perfect in all of Your ways. Help me to choose obedience to You even when I don't understand what You are doing or where You are leading. Amen.

*Day 45*

# WHEN REJECTION STINGS

> If the world hates you, keep in mind that it hated me first. If you belonged to the world, it would love you as its own. As it is, you do not belong to the world, but I have chosen you out of the world. That is why the world hates you.
>
> John 15:18–19

"I AM FREE *from being hindered by the fear of/sting of rejection."*

I go to youth camp as a leader every summer. Last year, during one of the services, we were provided with an index card and instructed to write down something that we had been freed from through the truth and power of God's Word and then encouraged to hold on to that card as a reminder. The above statement is what I wrote on mine.

One of the most threatening things to the enemy's plan to steal, kill, and destroy is to share the testimony of freedom you have found in Jesus. Freedom in Jesus is contagious. Throughout

**People's *rejection* cannot hinder God's *direction* for your life unless you allow it to.**

my life the sting of rejection has hindered me from stepping into the abundance of God's plan. I have, at times, allowed past experiences to steal present promises.

Maybe you are like me and putting your hope in people has failed you more times than you can count. Maybe someone else's doubt has caused you to second-guess what you know God said. Maybe you have been misunderstood because of your obedience to God's voice.

Know this: People may have rejected you, but Jesus never will. People's rejection cannot hinder God's direction for your life unless you allow it to. Live in the freedom and security of that promise. Life is far too short and God's plan for your life is far too good to allow past experiences, fear, or the opinion of others to delay you or keep you from walking in the freedom and abundance of following Jesus.

I know the pain of rejection is real, but the hope of Jesus is far greater than the pain you will experience. He won't leave you broken if you run to Him. He will comfort you, redeem what seems lost, and strengthen and guide you along the path of His perfect plan for your life. He will lead others into freedom through your willingness to share your testimony.

The beauty in the pain is His glory being revealed through it. It's an opportunity to look back to see and share the undeniable evidence of His faithfulness. Rejection may sting, but He is faithful to redeem. You are seen, known, and loved by Him, and nothing will ever change that.

> Fear of man will prove to be a snare,
> but whoever trusts in the Lord is kept safe.
> **Proverbs 29:25**

**REFLECTION AND APPLICATION:** How has rejection affected you personally? What have you been freed from that God might be challenging you to share to help someone else? What fear, anxiety, or worry does the truth from today's devotional replace?

**PRAYER:** Jesus, there is freedom from the fear of rejection in You. Help me to put my hope and confidence in You. Amen.

*Day 46*

# RESPOND WITH WORSHIP

> I will praise the LORD at all times.
> I will constantly speak his praises.
> I will boast only in the LORD;
> let all who are helpless take heart.
> Come, let us tell of the LORD's greatness;
> let us exalt his name together.
>
> Psalm 34:1–3 NLT

**LIVING A LIFESTYLE** of worship is one of the most effective remedies to anxiety. I am not suggesting that worship eliminates all worry from our lives, but it shifts our perspective from our problem to our solution, our Savior. We were created for worship, not just in a corporate setting but by continually walking with Jesus and putting before us a desire to honor Him in all that we say and do. Life pulls us in many directions and puts many distractions in our way. We need to be continually reminded to turn away from those distractions and turn toward Him.

**On your *best* and your *worst* day, Jesus is *worthy* of your worship.**

When we do what we are made for, it turns things around—if not our circumstances, then the way we respond to them. I love the fact that worship is for God's glory, but He is kind enough to allow us to be fulfilled and encouraged as we glorify Him. When our concerns and problems feel consuming, worship is a reminder of the One who is in control of everything we are concerned about. He is worthy of our praise in all things.

Today, fix your eyes on Jesus instead of your issues. Respond to whatever you are facing or feeling with worship. Regardless of what you are walking through, declare, "Yet I will praise Him." Thank Him for who He is, what He has done, and all that is to come. While it may not remove your worry, it will restore hope and confidence in His sovereignty. On your best and your worst day, Jesus is worthy of your worship. Today is a good day to do what you are made for, regardless of how you feel. Trust Him to do what only He can do.

> Through him then let us continually offer up a sacrifice of praise to God, that is, the fruit of lips that acknowledge his name.
>
> **Hebrews 13:15 ESV**

**REFLECTION AND APPLICATION:** How does worship change your perspective when you are worried? What does it mean to live a lifestyle of worship? What fear, anxiety, or worry does the truth from today's devotional replace?

**PRAYER:** Jesus, I commit to living a lifestyle of worship. When worship doesn't change my circumstances, remind me that it changes my heart and my perspective. You are worthy of my praise on my best and worst day. Amen.

*Day 47*

# CONSIDER THE WILDFLOWERS

Consider how the wild flowers grow. They do not labor or spin. Yet I tell you, not even Solomon in all his splendor was dressed like one of these. If that is how God clothes the grass of the field, which is here today, and tomorrow is thrown into the fire, how much more will he clothe you—you of little faith! And do not set your heart on what you will eat or drink; do not worry about it. For the pagan world runs after all such things, and your Father knows that you need them.

Luke 12:27–30

TO BE HONEST, I've read this passage for many years and have been frustrated because the peace it speaks of has always felt so unattainable. Maybe you can relate. I have wrestled with wondering how God could suggest I live a life so free of concern by calling me to consider things without a mind of their own. *Of course wildflowers don't worry*, I've thought. *They have nothing to worry about!*

My perspective recently changed when my husband and I were on a road trip. For many miles all there was to see were fields of wildflowers. As I watched them simply be, I was reminded of this passage, and I invited God to change my heart and help me to understand what it means to consider the wildflowers.

He wants me to live with such confidence that He will take care of me that worry cannot consume me or steal the abundance of life He has for me. We have minds, yes, but we can make up our minds to trust who He is and what He says. We can stand on His Word in such a way that we will not be swayed when we face uncertainty.

Wildflowers don't strive. They don't compete. They don't compare. They are simply what they have been created to be.

This passage is simply an invitation to trust. It is a promise to take care of us.

It's an invitation to rest. It's an encouragement to rely. It's a call to lay down striving and to experience the life of freedom and abundance He intended for those who will take Him at His Word.

Like the wildflowers, be the evidence to the world around you of a life of wholehearted dependence on Jesus.

We can *stand* on His Word in such a way that we will not be swayed when we face *uncertainty*.

> Why, you do not even know what will happen tomorrow. What is your life? You are a mist that appears for a little while and then vanishes. Instead, you ought to say, "If it is the Lord's will, we will live and do this or that."
>
> **James 4:14–15**

**REFLECTION AND APPLICATION:** What can you learn about trusting Jesus from the wildflowers? How will your life be different from the world around you when you depend on Him? What fear, anxiety, or worry does the truth from today's devotional replace?

**PRAYER:** Jesus, remind me to consider the wildflowers when it comes to trusting You. I want to live according to Your will, free of worry and full of confidence that You will take care of me. Amen.

*Day 48*

# FRIEND

No longer do I call you servants, for the servant does not know what his master is doing; but I have called you friends, for all that I have heard from my Father I have made known to you.

John 15:15 ESV

I THINK WE CAN ALL be guilty of putting Jesus in a box in our attempts to understand Him. No matter how hard we try, we cannot limit a limitless God by our own understanding or expectations. It's important that, even in our limited grasp, we open our hearts and minds to experience and accept all of who He is. He is Savior, Lord, Father . . . the list goes on and on. His Word is clear that He is also friend—and not just a friend but the most loyal, unfailing, and compassionate friend.

This character trait of God is significant for many reasons. One of the greatest fears most of us face is being alone. The friend we have in Jesus saves us from this fear. No matter how lonely we may feel, we are never alone. In earthly friendships, we will both

One of the greatest fears most of us face is being *alone*. The *friend* we have in Jesus saves us from this fear.

fail and be failed many times over, but to fail us is not in Jesus's nature. He upholds His promise to never leave us nor forsake us.

Our friend Jesus is near.

Our friend Jesus is compassionate and understanding.

Our friend Jesus not only meets us where we are but makes us better.

Our friend Jesus is intentional and involved.

Our friend Jesus is selfless.

Our friend Jesus is humble.

Our friend Jesus cared so much that He gave His own life to restore the relationship where sin once separated us from Him. There is no greater love. He doesn't just instruct us to be a friend; He sets the perfect example of how to live that friendship out.

Our friend Jesus is not just loving; He Himself is love. Open your heart to getting to know Him more as a friend today. He is the One we are created to long for and the One we should desire to be more like in all that we do.

> A man of many companions may come to ruin,
> but there is a friend who sticks closer than a brother.
> **Proverbs 18:24 ESV**

**REFLECTION AND APPLICATION:** What does it mean to you that Jesus calls you friend? What can we learn from His example about being a good friend? What fear, anxiety, or worry does the truth from today's devotional replace?

**PRAYER:** Jesus, thank You for calling me friend. Because You call me friend, I am never alone. Teach me to be more like You in all that I do. Amen.

*Day 49*

# RENEWED MIND

> Do not conform to the pattern of this world, but be transformed by the renewing of your mind. Then you will be able to test and approve what God's will is—his good, pleasing and perfect will.
>
> Romans 12:2

IT'S WILD, REALLY, the downward spiral that our minds can think us into. One thought leads to another, then another, and the next thing we know we are completely consumed with worry and can't even remember where it all began. The majority of the time, though, what we are worried about is bizarre or unrealistic. Sound familiar?

Our minds are powerful. They tell us what to believe and how to respond based on information they receive. I don't understand it all, but I do know that our thoughts form patterns, and those patterns create pathways that direct the way we feel, guide the decisions we make, and ultimately determine the lives that we live. With that said, it's safe to say that what we fill our minds with really does control us.

> Instead of being *controlled* by our fluctuating thoughts and emotions, we must *yield* to what He has spoken.

Scripture says we have been given a Spirit of power, love, and a sound mind (see 2 Tim. 1:7 NKJV). But how do we have a sound mind when our thoughts are so constant and chaotic? How can we fill our minds with good things when we see and experience bad things that we have no control over? Our thought patterns must be interrupted. Our minds must be rescued and renewed to ultimately save us from ourselves. The pathway to truth must be paved by God. Our thoughts must be continually and intentionally replaced with the truth of His Word. Instead of being controlled by our fluctuating thoughts and emotions, we must yield to what He has spoken.

With each morning, His mercies are new, and in every moment we are provided an opportunity to be transformed by the renewing of our minds. A sound mind is a renewed mind. A sound mind is a transformed mind. A sound mind is a mind that trusts God and takes Him at His Word.

Invite Jesus to invade your thoughts. Allow Him to transform your way of thinking. Ask Him to move you from conforming to the pattern of the world to living in obedience to His Word in your thoughts, words, and actions. Through your obedience, He will lead you along the path of His perfect plan for your life.

> Therefore, with minds that are alert and fully sober, set your hope on the grace to be brought to you when Jesus Christ is revealed at his coming.
>
> **1 Peter 1:13**

**REFLECTION AND APPLICATION:** What reoccurring thoughts need to be renewed and transformed by the truth of His Word? What fear, anxiety, or worry does the truth from today's devotional replace?

**PRAYER:** Jesus, continually renew my mind and transform me through the truth of Your Word. Direct me in identifying and following Your good, pleasing, and perfect will for my life. Amen.

## *Day 50*

# NOTHING CAN SEPARATE

> Therefore, there is now no condemnation for those who are in Christ Jesus, because through Christ Jesus the law of the Spirit who gives life has set you free from the law of sin and death.
>
> Romans 8:1–2

I AM AWARE of the shame that attempts to attach itself to the fear, anxiety, and worry we have. Not only does the enemy want us to fear but he wants to trap us in feelings of shame and guilt too. He wants our fears and failures to cause us to run and hide from Jesus instead of run to Him. The enemy wants to keep us from freedom and convince us that we are victims.

There is a truth in God's Word for every lie the enemy whispers in attempts to distract, discourage, and defeat you and keep you from stepping deeper into relationship with Jesus. The closer you are to Jesus, the more of a threat you become to the enemy. First

> The *closer* you are to Jesus, the more of a *threat* you become to the enemy.

and foremost, you need to know that nothing can separate you from the love of God.

Romans 8:38–39 says, "For I am convinced that neither death nor life, neither angels nor demons, neither the present nor the future, nor any powers, neither height nor depth, nor anything else in all creation, will be able to separate us from the love of God that is in Christ Jesus our Lord."

Live convinced of this truth—that nothing can separate you from the love of Christ. Let your fears and failures send you running to Him, not from Him. While the enemy tries to keep you captive, Jesus came to set you free from fear and shame and everything that keeps you distant from Him. Where the enemy comes to steal, kill, and destroy, Jesus came to give you life abundant.

Because of Christ, you are not a victim to sin or shame; you are victorious. Walk in liberty. Live in the light of His truth and let the power of His love do what only it can do in your life.

> There is no fear in love, but perfect love casts out fear. For fear has to do with punishment, and whoever fears has not been perfected in love.
>
> **1 John 4:18 ESV**

**REFLECTION AND APPLICATION:** Why does fear often lead to feelings of shame? What is the importance of living in confidence that nothing can separate you from the love of Jesus? What fear, anxiety, or worry does the truth from today's devotional replace?

**PRAYER:** Jesus, thank You for the promise that nothing can separate me from Your love. Let me live in the light of Your truth that sets me free from fear and shame. Amen.

# Day 51

# CELEBRATE

This is the day the Lord has made.
We will rejoice and be glad in it.
Psalm 118:24 NLT

ONE OF THE MOST valuable things I was taught throughout my childhood and beyond was the power of celebration. My family consistently practiced celebrating small victories instead of waiting for the next "big" moment to rejoice and give thanks. It helped me to understand that there is something to be celebrated every day, and it encouraged me to practice obedience to Scripture's instruction to rejoice continually (see 1 Thess. 5:16).

Here's the thing—continual celebration breeds contentment. And contentment protects us from comparison and results in a lifestyle of gratitude. Comparison causes competition, striving, and anxiety. It keeps us in a cycle of attempting to keep up with culture's standard of success. Gratitude leads us to celebration, rest, and a settled heart. A life of wishing, wanting, and striving for what we don't have is not the life Jesus intended for His

**Contentment protects us from comparison and results in a lifestyle of gratitude.**

people. He calls us to so much more, to live with an eternal idea of success.

We are called to rejoice and invited to live in awareness of God's goodness and kindness all around us. It's good for our hearts to give thanks for what we have been given and to dwell in His promises, which are yes and Amen (see 2 Cor. 1:20). This doesn't mean we can't have desires or ask for things according to His will, but it does mean we are called to ultimately rest in the fact that, in Him, we really do have all that we need. This is why He tells us to be anxious for nothing all throughout the Bible.

Abundance is not attainable outside of celebration. Rejoicing always is a vital part of walking in God's will, and it will transform your life. This is the day that He has made. If you stop for a moment to look, you will see that there are reasons to rejoice all around, regardless of what you are walking through.

> Rejoice always, pray continually, give thanks in all circumstances; for this is God's will for you in Christ Jesus.
>
> **1 Thessalonians 5:16–18**

**REFLECTION AND APPLICATION:** What are some reasons you have to rejoice today? Why is celebration crucial to living a life of contentment that is free from anxiety? What fear, anxiety, or worry does the truth from today's devotional replace?

**PRAYER:** Jesus, thank You for Your goodness and kindness. Help me to live a life of contentment through continual celebration. I lay down wishing, striving, and wanting and pick up gratitude and rejoicing. Amen.

*Day 52*

# BE STILL + KNOW

The LORD will fight for you; you need only to be still.

Exodus 14:14

WE DON'T LIKE TO BE STILL, and we aren't good at it either, especially when we are fearful. Our nature is to panic. To rush. To attempt to take matters into our own hands and hold on tight to control as much as we can. Many spend their days consumed by chaos, confusion, and uncertainty. There is a common theme throughout Scripture that contradicts our way of doing things. Amid our tendency to live overwhelmed with worry, we are interrupted with an invitation that goes against our instincts.

> Be still, and know that I am God;
> I will be exalted among the nations,
> I will be exalted in the earth.
>
> **Psalm 46:10**

This stillness is not referring to the physical definition of the word, though listening to this instruction will cause us to slow

To be *still* and *know* that He is God is to have a settled *heart* and *mind* even when surrounded by chaos.

down. This kind of stillness is a result of living in awareness of who God is and holding on to His promises. To be still and know that He is God is to have a settled heart and mind even when surrounded by chaos. It's to know that our lives are better off in His hands than in our own. Living in this awareness will move us from striving to surrender, from panic to peace, from rushing to reliance, and from fear to confident trust.

One of the most amazing things about this stillness is that it will stand out in a world that does not know Jesus. While others tremble in fear, you will be recognized for the peace that trusting in Him produces within you. Your response to what would cause others to panic will point others to Him.

The chaos you experience and the feelings you navigate provide you with everyday opportunities to not only know that He is God but to live like you believe it. When you are tempted to fight or to flee, be still and know that He is God—and that He is sovereign over every circumstance.

> Be still before the Lord
> and wait patiently for him;
> do not fret when people succeed in their ways,
> when they carry out their wicked schemes.
>
> **Psalm 37:7**

**REFLECTION AND APPLICATION:** What does it look like to be still and know that He is God? How will your life stand out when you live in confidence in His sovereignty? What fear, anxiety, or worry does the truth from today's devotional replace?

**PRAYER:** Jesus, instead of taking matters into my own hands, lead me to be still and know that You are God. Replace my worry and panic with a settled heart and mind. Amen.

*Day 53*

# FINDING PURPOSE

The Lord will fulfill his purpose for me;
your steadfast love, O Lord, endures forever.
Do not forsake the work of your hands.

Psalm 138:8 ESV

**I HAVE SPENT** a lot of time throughout my life confused about and unsure of my purpose. I live in the tension of what is my part and what is God's. This psalm makes it clear that I am not the fulfiller of my purpose—God is. It's not up to me to fulfill my purpose—it's up to Him.

I am responsible for giving God my yes (in words, heart, and action) and trusting Him to order my steps on the mundane days and extraordinary days alike. The longer I walk with Jesus, the more my perspective about my purpose is transformed. Instead of spending my time trying to figure out and establish my own purpose, I am called to spend my life in pursuit of the Purpose Fulfiller, Promise Keeper, and Waymaker.

Ultimately, He is our purpose. He is our calling. He should be our greatest treasure.

**The One who has *called* you is the same One who equips and *qualifies* you.**

Our primary purpose is to pursue Him. The rest of the details of our lives are safe in His hands and with the help of His guidance. Ask Him to identify the gifts He has given you and the doors He has opened for you, even if they aren't your most preferred position or what you think is your passion. Start with stewarding those things to the best of your ability—intentionally, consistently, and faithfully trusting what His Word says. In the process, He will make clear what is confusing.

He guides us in a way that reminds us of our need for Him all along. If we have everything we have ever dreamed of but lack Him, we are left with nothing at all.

Pursue the Purpose (and Promise) Fulfiller. The One who has called you is the same One who equips and qualifies you. You don't try your way into kingdom success; you surrender your way into kingdom success. Do what He has called you to do, and He will do with your life what only He can do so that it all points back to His glory.

It starts and ends with pursuing Him.

> For God saved us and called us to live a holy life. He did this, not because we deserved it, but because that was his plan from before the beginning of time—to show us his grace through Christ Jesus.
>
> **2 Timothy 1:9 NLT**

**REFLECTION AND APPLICATION:** How does Psalm 138:8 change your view of your responsibility in discovering your purpose? What fear, anxiety, or worry does the truth from today's devotional replace?

**PRAYER:** Jesus, I know that my first priority should be pursuing You. I surrender striving for following You and trusting You to fulfill Your purpose for me. Amen.

# Day 54

# THE BETTER WAY

God's way is perfect.
All the LORD's promises prove true.
He is a shield for all who look to him for protection.

2 Samuel 22:31 NLT

IF MY TRUST IN JESUS was built on Him doing things my way, I would have walked away a long time ago. Friend, He sympathizes with us in our disappointment when it doesn't unravel how we thought or hoped it would.

He leads us on with this gentle whisper, "You don't understand now, but one day you will. It's all for your good. Trust Me."

My confidence in Jesus has been developed over time through His faithfulness prevailing over my failed plans. Disappointment, discouragement, waiting—only for Him to show up right on time in just the way I need time and time again. Now, more often than I am disappointed when things don't go as planned, I recognize that those upsets pave a path for His way, which is better. Trusting in Him doesn't mean there will be no disappointment or pain

Trusting Him is the *adventure* of a lifetime.

in the process; it just means He has a plan beyond those moments of pain and disappointment and that that plan will prevail as I surrender to His leadership.

Our Good Shepherd has never not been faithful. He doesn't intend to start with you or me, no matter how much we convince ourselves that we must be the exception to His faithfulness, that God must have forgotten what He has spoken, that He really should do it our way.

I can't tell you exactly what His plan is for your life, or the process in which it will all unfold—I can't even identify that for my own life. And you know what? That is exactly where He wants us to reside, where we are required to trust Him consistently and confidently for His glory to most be revealed in and through our lives.

There will be moments and times where it will seem like He has failed us or forgotten we exist, but He will not leave us in the disappointment of our current circumstances. He will show up at the right time because He can be trusted to orchestrate every detail of your life. Trusting Him is the adventure of a lifetime.

> Jesus replied, "You do not realize now what I am doing, but later you will understand."
>
> **John 13:7**

**REFLECTION AND APPLICATION:** How have you seen God's faithfulness prevail over your failed plans? Where do you currently feel failed or forgotten, and how can you trust Him in those areas? What fear, anxiety, or worry does the truth from today's devotional replace?

**PRAYER:** Jesus, I trust that Your way is perfect. When my plans fail, remind me that Yours will prevail and that You work all things together for my good. Amen.

*Day 55*

# AUTHOR + FINISHER

> And I am certain that God, who began the good work within you, will continue his work until it is finally finished on the day when Christ Jesus returns.
>
> Philippians 1:6 NLT

**YOUR STORY** is being written by the greatest author, who is aware of your every need, want, and deepest desire. You are held in the palm of His mighty hand, and there is no safer place to be than seen, known, and loved by Him. He has worked out everything you are worried about before the thought even enters your mind. He goes before and behind you and surrounds you.

How freeing is it to allow your weary heart to find rest in this truth? It will allow you to look forward in hope and expectation that He is in control.

Though we are so quick to forget it, He is gracious to remind us that there is no need to worry about tomorrow or attempt to orchestrate the outcome, because He is preparing and paving

**What we wish could be left out, He uses for *good*. What we wish we could erase, instead He *redeems*.**

the way. As we walk with Him, He hears our cries, considers our feelings, and remains close. He has us, and though that truth is easier to proclaim than to believe and live out confidently, the more we proclaim it and continue to step forward in faith, the more our trust in Him will grow as He reveals His faithfulness.

The pen of our stories is better in His hand than in our own. What we wish could be left out, He uses for good. What we wish we could erase, instead He redeems. His goodness is woven like a thread through every chapter and page, and while it is easier to follow sometimes than others, it never fails. Though our stories are different, they are all the same in this way.

He does not leave stories unfinished. The work He began, He will complete—for your good and His glory. Through your life, the story of His faithfulness through generations is continuing to be written and revealed to a world that desperately needs Him.

> Fixing our eyes on Jesus, the pioneer and perfecter of faith. For the joy set before him he endured the cross, scorning its shame, and sat down at the right hand of the throne of God.
>
> **Hebrews 12:2**

**REFLECTION AND APPLICATION:** Why is the story of your life better off in His hands than in your own? Reflect on the evidence of His goodness that you can currently identify in your life. What fear, anxiety, or worry does the truth from today's devotional replace?

**PRAYER:** Jesus, I acknowledge You as the perfect Author and Finisher of my story. Use my life to reveal Your goodness and glory. Amen.

## *Day 56*

# GOOD NEWS

Surely the righteous will never be shaken;
  they will be remembered forever.
They will have no fear of bad news;
  their hearts are steadfast, trusting in the LORD.
Their hearts are secure, they will have no fear;
  in the end they will look in triumph on their foes.

Psalm 112:6–8

ANXIETY CAUSES US to constantly expect the worst-case scenario. Trusting in Jesus allows our hearts to anticipate His goodness in all things. Living in fear causes us to constantly brace for bad news. Living in faith leads us to put our hope in who He is and what He has promised. When you attempt to find security in your circumstances, you will be swayed, but as long as you put your confidence in Jesus, you will not be shaken.

The good news given to those who trust Him far outweighs any bad news we might fear or face. The good news is that the One we have placed our confidence in promises to work all things together for the good of those who love Him. He gives beauty

> As long as you put your *confidence* in Jesus, you will not be *shaken*.

for ashes and joy for mourning. He never fails. He uses everything we experience to increase our confidence in His faithfulness and our dependence on Him.

When you find yourself worried and full of fear of bad news, remember what He has promised. Remember who He is and hold on to the promise that His Word is unfailing and unchanging. Walk in the reward of righteousness—free of the constant fear of bad news and full of expectation for Him to not only meet but exceed your expectations!

No matter at what point in the story you find yourself, it ends in victory for those who love and live in obedience to Him. He will keep you secure as you trust Him. This is GOOD NEWS.

> To all who mourn in Israel,
> he will give a crown of beauty for ashes,
> a joyous blessing instead of mourning,
> festive praise instead of despair.
> In their righteousness, they will be like great oaks
> that the Lord has planted for his own glory.
>
> **Isaiah 61:3 NLT**

**REFLECTION AND APPLICATION:** What does Psalm 112:6–8 teach you about trusting Jesus? Where have you expected the worst-case scenario that you need to replace with anticipation for His goodness and faithfulness? What fear, anxiety, or worry does the truth from today's devotional replace?

**PRAYER:** Jesus, I don't want to live in constant fear of bad news. Keep my heart steadfast, anticipating Your goodness in all things. Amen.

# *Day 57*

# SURRENDERED STEPS

> And those who belong to Christ Jesus have crucified the flesh with its passions and desires. If we live by the Spirit, let us also keep in step with the Spirit.
>
> Galatians 5:24–25 ESV

IF YOU FEAR you are falling behind in life, remember this: Surrender may not lead you as fast and as far as you want to go from the perspective of earthly success, but it keeps you in step with the One who has the best plan for your life.

I wholeheartedly believe (and am living proof) that God wants to and will bless us, and that His plans for us are so good. But He is most concerned with us becoming more like Him. True fulfillment is found only in knowing and following Jesus.

I am learning that I don't need to know as much as I think to move forward in what God has called me to. Does anyone remember the song "Following the Leader" from *Peter Pan*? It says we follow wherever the leader may go. That's it. We don't always have to know where we are going, what step to take next, or what to do. We simply must stay in step with the One we are following . . . wherever He leads.

I recognize that some of you may be in seasons where you have decisions to make or are seeking clarity on what steps to take. My encouragement to you would be to diligently seek the One you are following above all else. Live a life of obedience to Him.

Sometimes He will give you very specific directions. Other times, you will have to step forward and decide or go in a direction with a simple desire to honor Him in all that you do.

In a culture that's saturated by social media, it's easy to associate following Jesus with these big, extravagant moments. There's a place for those moments, but often, following Him looks like the simple and mundane. It looks like the decisions made when no one else is watching. It's all miraculous because of who He is.

Be less consumed with the "what," "where," and "when" and be more consumed with the "who" it's all about. As you remain uncompromising in your decision to follow Jesus (living in obedience to His Word and His voice), you will look back and see His faithfulness in ordering your every step—even when you felt like you lacked clarity and felt you were behind.

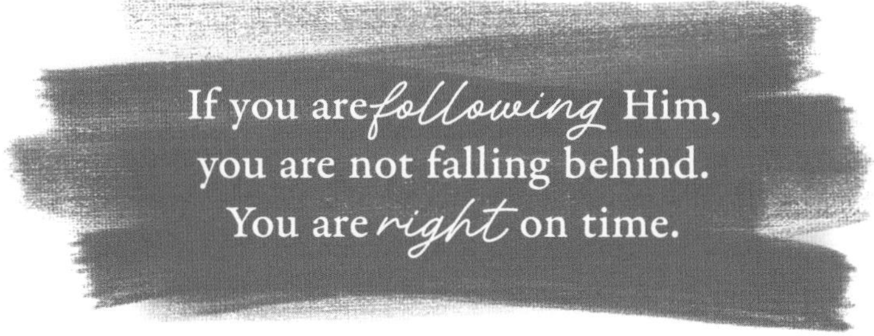

Follow Him, wherever He leads. If you are following Him, you are not falling behind. You are right on time.

> Many are the plans in a person's heart,
> but it is the LORD's purpose that prevails.
> **Proverbs 19:21**

**REFLECTION AND APPLICATION:** How does surrendering to Jesus protect you from the pressure to "keep up"? Where have you turned to your own strategy that you need to surrender to Him? What fear, anxiety, or worry does the truth from today's devotional replace?

**PRAYER:** Jesus, direct me in living a life of surrender, following wherever You lead. Thank You for the promise that when I am following You, I will not be misled or fall behind. Amen.

## *Day 58*

# RELY

> The Lord will guide you always;
> he will satisfy your needs in a sun-scorched land
> and will strengthen your frame.
> You will be like a well-watered garden,
> like a spring whose waters never fail.
>
> Isaiah 58:11

R*ELY* IS MY WORD for the year. It means "to depend on with full trust or confidence." I know full well that it is easy to set our minds up in the camp of all kinds of fears and unknowns. In this case, the easy option is not the better option. Instead of living consumed by fear, we are invited to build our lives on the confidence that Jesus is in control. He has instructed us to trust Him with everything in every moment of every day.

A life of surrender is a life of continual reliance. A life of reliance results in the rest that is found only in and through Jesus. Reliance means to trust Him wholeheartedly. He doesn't want our partial trust. He wants us to fully depend on Him in every area of our

**A life of *reliance* results in the rest that is found *only* in and through Jesus.**

lives. A life of faith, which is needed to please Him, requires a life of complete confidence in who He is and dependence on Him.

Be careful not to live a life just claiming that you trust Jesus; make sure that your life reflects that trust. When you are tempted to operate according to your own understanding, remember that both His plan and His understanding are unfailing. Invite Him to do things His way and according to His will in every area of your life.

Choose surrender.

Choose obedience.

Choose His perfect plan over your preference.

Rely on Him every day, every moment, every hour, and every second.

Do what He has asked of you and let Him do the rest.

He is with you, He is for you, and His plans for you are good.

> Trust in *and* rely confidently on the Lord with all your heart
> And do not rely on your own insight *or* understanding.
>
> In all your ways know *and* acknowledge *and* recognize Him,
> And He will make your paths straight *and* smooth
> [removing obstacles that block your way].
>
> **Proverbs 3:5–6 AMP**

**REFLECTION AND APPLICATION:** What does it mean to reflect your reliance on Jesus? In what area(s) are you currently not relying on Him? What fear, anxiety, or worry does the truth from today's devotional replace?

**PRAYER:** Jesus, help me to depend on You with full trust and confidence. Thank You for guiding, providing for, and protecting me as I continually rely on You. Amen.

*Day 59*

# HOPE

> I pray that God, the source of hope, will fill you completely with joy and peace because you trust in him. Then you will overflow with confident hope through the power of the Holy Spirit.
>
> Romans 15:13 NLT

WHEN OUR MINDS wander and our hearts stray, grace gently draws us back in and reminds us that hope is available to all who receive it because Jesus is alive!

The hope available to us through Him is not wishful thinking; it is the promise of His faithfulness provided to us to hold fast to in every season, situation, and circumstance. The world cannot take this hope because the world did not provide this hope.

It is bright on the horizon of every mountain high and valley low and every step of the way on the journey in between.

It is present in both deep sorrow and great rejoicing.

It triumphs over every defeat and disappointment we face.

This hope we have is not empty, distant, or dependent on what our eyes can see in a moment.

We have this *hope* to hold on to that won't ever let us go. His *name* is Jesus.

It remains fully present and active when things appear hopeless in our sight.

We have this anchor when the waves of the world are crashing all around us.

We have this confidence and assurance when uncertainty is surrounding us.

We have this faith that remains, despite the many reasons it seems that we have to doubt and fear.

We have this confidence about how the story ends when we find ourselves overwhelmed by the in-between.

It ends in victory for those who put their trust in Jesus. Walking in the assurance of what He has promised never has and never will lead to disappointment.

We have this hope to hold on to that won't ever let us go. His name is Jesus. In the face of every fear, worry, and anxiety, hope is never lost. Return to the hope you have in Him and allow Him to replace your fears with the truth of His Word that sets us free.

> Let us hold fast the confession of our hope without wavering, for he who promised is faithful.
>
> **Hebrews 10:23 ESV**

**REFLECTION AND APPLICATION:** What does the promise of hope in Jesus mean to you? The world cannot rob you of the hope you have in Him—how is that significant for you personally? What fear, anxiety, or worry does the truth from today's devotional replace?

**PRAYER:** Jesus, thank You for the unfailing hope I have in You. Increase my confidence in the fact that placing my hope in You every day will not lead to disappointment. Amen.

## *Day 60*

# SEARCHED + KNOWN

> My sheep listen to my voice; I know them, and they follow me.
>
> John 10:27

AS I PRAYED about what to share on the final day, it felt fitting to leave you with a passage of Scripture that has been personally transformative in replacing my fear, worry, and anxieties with the truth of God's Word. While I hope my words have been an encouragement to you, I want to remind you that His truth is the best place to run to. It's the only thing that truly sets us free. For some of you, these words will be familiar. For others of you, they will be new. Either way, I pray they bring you comfort and lead you to rest in and rely on Jesus.

> You have searched me, LORD,
>     and you know me.
> You know when I sit and when I rise;
>     you perceive my thoughts from afar.

You discern my going out and my lying down;
    you are familiar with all my ways.
Before a word is on my tongue
    you, Lord, know it completely.
You hem me in behind and before,
    and you lay your hand upon me.
Such knowledge is too wonderful for me,
    too lofty for me to attain.

Where can I go from your Spirit?
    Where can I flee from your presence?
If I go up to the heavens, you are there;
    if I make my bed in the depths, you are there.
If I rise on the wings of the dawn,
    if I settle on the far side of the sea,
even there your hand will guide me,
    your right hand will hold me fast.
If I say, "Surely the darkness will hide me
    and the light become night around me,"
even the darkness will not be dark to you;
    the night will shine like the day,
    for darkness is as light to you.

For you created my inmost being;
    you knit me together in my mother's womb.
I praise you because I am fearfully and wonderfully made;
    your works are wonderful,
    I know that full well.
My frame was not hidden from you
    when I was made in the secret place,
    when I was woven together in the depths of the earth.
Your eyes saw my unformed body;
    all the days ordained for me were written in your book
    before one of them came to be.

How precious to me are your thoughts, God!
  How vast is the sum of them!
Were I to count them,
  they would outnumber the grains of sand—
  when I awake, I am still with you.

If only you, God, would slay the wicked!
  Away from me, you who are bloodthirsty!
They speak of you with evil intent;
  your adversaries misuse your name.
Do I not hate those who hate you, LORD,
  and abhor those who are in rebellion against you?
I have nothing but hatred for them;
  I count them my enemies.
Search me, God, and know my heart;
  test me and know my anxious thoughts.
See if there is any offensive way in me,
  and lead me in the way everlasting.

**Psalm 139:1–24**

**REFLECTION AND APPLICATION:** In what ways have fear, anxiety, and worry been replaced with the truth of God's Word in your life over the last sixty days? Take some time to reflect.

**PRAYER:** Jesus, in the days to come, I will continue to trust the truth of Your Word over my fears, anxieties, and worries. Help me to rest in and rely on You in all that I do all the days of my life. Amen.

## CLOSING PRAYER

*Jesus, thank You for increasing my understanding of who You are and my understanding of Your truth, which frees me from anything that hinders the abundance You have for me. I recognize that overcoming fear is not accomplished through trying harder in my own strength but resting in and relying on Your strength and power at work within me. When I am afraid and overwhelmed, I will put my trust in You. In the days ahead, continue to guide me in replacing every fear, worry, and anxious thought with confidence in Your promises. Remind me every step of the way that You are always with me and will never fail me. Use my life to reveal Your goodness and glory. Amen.*

## SALVATION PRAYER

*Jesus, I recognize that I have sinned and fallen short of Your standard, and I ask You to forgive me. I believe that You are the Son of God, that You died to pay the price for the sins that I could never repay, and that You rose again three days later. I invite You into my heart and surrender my life to You from this day forward. Thank You for the gift of grace and the guidance of Your Spirit. Help me to know, trust, and follow You. Amen.*

# SCRIPTURE REFERENCE GUIDE

But the eyes of the Lord are on those who fear him,
on those whose hope is in his unfailing love.

**Psalm 33:18**

Then she called the name of the Lord who spoke to her, "You are God Who Sees"; for she said, "Have I not even here [in the wilderness] remained alive after seeing Him [who sees me with understanding and compassion]?"

**Genesis 16:13 AMP**

Are not two sparrows sold for a penny? Yet not one of them will fall to the ground outside your Father's care. And even the very hairs of your head are all numbered. So don't be afraid; you are worth more than many sparrows.

**Matthew 10:29–31**

So do not fear, for I am with you;
do not be dismayed, for I am your God.
I will strengthen you and help you;
I will uphold you with my righteous right hand.

**Isaiah 41:10**

And surely I am with you always, to the very end of the age.

**Matthew 28:20**

Jesus answered, "It is written: 'Man shall not live on bread alone, but on every word that comes from the mouth of God.'"

**Matthew 4:4**

The grass withers and the flowers fade,
but the word of our God stands forever.

**Isaiah 40:8 NLT**

We demolish arguments and every pretension that sets itself up against the knowledge of God, and we take captive every thought to make it obedient to Christ.

**2 Corinthians 10:5**

It is for freedom that Christ has set us free. Stand firm, then, and do not let yourselves be burdened again by a yoke of slavery.

**Galatians 5:1**

The Lord is my light and my salvation;
whom shall I fear?
The Lord is the stronghold of my life;
of whom shall I be afraid?

**Psalm 27:1 ESV**

I will say of the Lord, "He is my refuge and my fortress,
my God, in whom I trust."

**Psalm 91:2**

Jesus spoke to the people once more and said, "I am the light of the world. If you follow me, you won't have to walk in darkness, because you will have the light that leads to life."

**John 8:12 NLT**

You came near when I called you,
and you said, "Do not fear."
**Lamentations 3:57**

There is no fear in love. But perfect love drives out fear, because fear has to do with punishment. The one who fears is not made perfect in love.

**1 John 4:18**

My sheep listen to my voice; I know them, and they follow me.

**John 10:27**

Now Christ has gone to heaven. He is seated in the place of honor next to God, and all the angels and authorities and powers accept his authority.

**1 Peter 3:22 NLT**

Then Jesus came to them and said, "All authority in heaven and on earth has been given to me."

**Matthew 28:18**

So we say with confidence,

"The Lord is my helper; I will not be afraid.
What can mere mortals do to me?"
**Hebrews 13:6**

Have you never heard?
Have you never understood?
The Lord is the everlasting God,
the Creator of all the earth.

He never grows weak or weary.
No one can measure the depths of his understanding.

**Isaiah 40:28 NLT**

Show me your ways, Lord,
teach me your paths.
Guide me in your truth and teach me,
for you are God my Savior,
and my hope is in you all day long.

**Psalm 25:4–5**

I will instruct you and teach you in the way you should go;
I will counsel you with my loving eye on you.

**Psalm 32:8**

The heart of man plans his way,
but the Lord establishes his steps.

**Proverbs 16:9 ESV**

He renews my strength.
He guides me along right paths,
bringing honor to his name.

**Psalm 23:3 NLT**

If we confess our sins, he is faithful and just and will forgive us our sins and purify us from all unrighteousness.

**1 John 1:9**

"No longer will they teach their neighbor,
or say to one another, 'Know the Lord,'
because they will all know me,
from the least of them to the greatest,"
declares the Lord.

"For I will forgive their wickedness
and will remember their sins no more."
**Jeremiah 31:34**

He has removed our sins as far from us
as the east is from the west.
**Psalm 103:12 NLT**

Therefore, if anyone is in Christ, the new creation has come: The old has gone, the new is here!

**2 Corinthians 5:17**

Then Jesus said, "Come to me, all of you who are weary and carry heavy burdens, and I will give you rest. Take my yoke upon you. Let me teach you, because I am humble and gentle at heart, and you will find rest for your souls."

**Matthew 11:28–29 NLT**

The Lord replied, "My Presence will go with you, and I will give you rest."
**Exodus 33:14**

*When You said*, "Seek My face [in prayer, require My presence as your greatest need]," my heart said to You, "Your face, O Lord, I will seek [on the authority of Your word]."

**Psalm 27:8 AMP**

Look to the Lord and his strength;
seek his face always.
**1 Chronicles 16:11**

The Lord isn't really being slow about his promise, as some people think. No, he is being patient for your sake. He does not want anyone to be destroyed, but wants everyone to repent.

**2 Peter 3:9 NLT**

Lord, you are my God;
  I will exalt you and praise your name,
for in perfect faithfulness
  you have done wonderful things,
  things planned long ago.

**Isaiah 25:1**

The Lord is near to all who call on him,
  to all who call on him in truth.

**Psalm 145:18**

Where shall I go from your Spirit?
  Or where shall I flee from your presence?
If I ascend to heaven, you are there!
  If I make my bed in Sheol, you are there!
If I take the wings of the morning
  and dwell in the uttermost parts of the sea,
even there your hand shall lead me,
  and your right hand shall hold me.

**Psalm 139:7–10 ESV**

If we are faithless,
  he remains faithful,
  for he cannot disown himself.

**2 Timothy 2:13**

I will [solemnly] remember the deeds of the Lord;
Yes, I will [wholeheartedly] remember Your wonders of
  old.

**Psalm 77:11 AMP**

Let all that I am praise the Lord;
    may I never forget the good things he does for me.
**Psalm 103:2 NLT**

The mind governed by the flesh is death, but the mind governed by the Spirit is life and peace.

**Romans 8:6**

Set your minds on things above, not on earthly things.
**Colossians 3:2**

The Lord has established his throne in heaven,
    and his kingdom rules over all.
**Psalm 103:19**

He is before all things, and in him all things hold together.
**Colossians 1:17**

I make known the end from the beginning,
    from ancient times, what is still to come.
I say, "My purpose will stand,
    and I will do all that I please."
**Isaiah 46:10**

The Lord himself goes before you and will be with you; he will never leave you nor forsake you. Do not be afraid; do not be discouraged.
**Deuteronomy 31:8**

For I am the Lord your God
    who takes hold of your right hand
and says to you, Do not fear;
    I will help you.
**Isaiah 41:13**

Be strong and courageous. Do not be afraid or terrified because of them, for the Lord your God goes with you; he will never leave you nor forsake you.

**Deuteronomy 31:6**

Have I not commanded you? Be strong and courageous. Do not be afraid; do not be discouraged, for the Lord your God will be with you wherever you go.

**Joshua 1:9**

Wait patiently for the Lord.
Be brave and courageous.
Yes, wait patiently for the Lord.

**Psalm 27:14 NLT**

And now, dear brothers and sisters, one final thing. Fix your thoughts on what is true, and honorable, and right, and pure, and lovely, and admirable. Think about things that are excellent and worthy of praise.

**Philippians 4:8 NLT**

You will keep in perfect peace
all who trust in you,
all whose thoughts are fixed on you!

**Isaiah 26:3 NLT**

May the God of hope fill you with all joy and peace as you trust in him, so that you may overflow with hope by the power of the Holy Spirit.

**Romans 15:13**

And I will ask the Father, and he will give you another advocate to help you and be with you forever. . . . But the Advocate, the Holy Spirit, whom the Father will send in my name, will teach you all things and will remind you of everything I have said to you.

**John 14:16, 26**

For his anger lasts only a moment,
but his favor lasts a lifetime;
weeping may stay for the night,
but rejoicing comes in the morning.

**Psalm 30:5**

"Blessed [with spiritual security] is the man who believes
*and* trusts in *and* relies on the LORD
And whose hope *and* confident expectation is the LORD.

"For he will be [nourished] like a tree planted by the
waters,
That spreads out its roots by the river;
And will not fear the heat when it comes;
But its leaves will be green *and* moist.
And it will not be anxious *and* concerned in a year of
drought
Nor stop bearing fruit."

**Jeremiah 17:7–8 AMP**

Indeed, the very hairs of your head are all numbered. Don't be afraid; you are worth more than many sparrows.

**Luke 12:7**

My flesh and my heart may fail,
but God is the strength of my heart
and my portion forever.

**Psalm 73:26**

Remember how the Lord your God led you all the way in the wilderness these forty years, to humble and test you in order to know what was in your heart, whether or not you would keep his commands.

**Deuteronomy 8:2**

You, God, are my God,
earnestly I seek you;
I thirst for you,
my whole being longs for you,
in a dry and parched land
where there is no water.

I have seen you in the sanctuary
and beheld your power and your glory.
Because your love is better than life,
my lips will glorify you.
I will praise you as long as I live,
and in your name I will lift up my hands.
I will be fully satisfied as with the richest of foods;
with singing lips my mouth will praise you.

On my bed I remember you;
I think of you through the watches of the night.
Because you are my help,
I sing in the shadow of your wings.
I cling to you;
your right hand upholds me.

Those who want to kill me will be destroyed;
they will go down to the depths of the earth.
They will be given over to the sword
and become food for jackals.

But the king will rejoice in God;
all who swear by God will glory in him,
while the mouths of liars will be silenced.

**Psalm 63**

I know what it is to be in need, and I know what it is to have plenty. I have learned the secret of being content in any and every situation, whether well fed or hungry, whether living in plenty or in want. I can do all this through him who gives me strength.

**Philippians 4:12–13**

Whether you turn to the right or to the left, your ears will hear a voice behind you, saying, "This is the way; walk in it."

**Isaiah 30:21**

You will decide on a matter, and it will be established for you,
and light will shine on your ways.

**Job 22:28 ESV**

Cast your burden on the Lord [release it] and He will sustain *and* uphold you; He will never allow the righteous to be shaken (slip, fall, fail).

**Psalm 55:22 AMP**

Cast all your anxiety on him because he cares for you.

**1 Peter 5:7**

Immediately after this, Jesus insisted that his disciples get back into the boat and cross to the other side of the lake, while he sent the people home. After sending them home, he went up into the hills by himself to pray. Night fell while he was there alone.

Meanwhile, the disciples were in trouble far away from land, for a strong wind had risen, and they were fighting heavy waves. About three o'clock in the morning Jesus came toward them, walking on the water. When the disciples saw him walking on the water, they were terrified. In their fear, they cried out, "It's a ghost!"

But Jesus spoke to them at once. "Don't be afraid," he said. "Take courage. I am here!"

Then Peter called to him, "Lord, if it's really you, tell me to come to you, walking on the water."

"Yes, come," Jesus said.

So Peter went over the side of the boat and walked on the water toward Jesus. But when he saw the strong wind and the waves, he was terrified and began to sink. "Save me, Lord!" he shouted.

Jesus immediately reached out and grabbed him. "You have so little faith," Jesus said. "Why did you doubt me?"

When they climbed back into the boat, the wind stopped. Then the disciples worshiped him. "You really are the Son of God!" they exclaimed.

**Matthew 14:22–33 NLT**

When you pass through the waters, I will be with you;
And through the rivers, they will not overwhelm you.
When you walk through fire, you will not be scorched,
Nor will the flame burn you.

**Isaiah 43:2 AMP**

The Lord makes firm the steps
of the one who delights in him;
though he may stumble, he will not fall,
for the Lord upholds him with his hand.

**Psalm 37:23–24**

"For I know the plans I have for you," declares the Lord, "plans to prosper you and not to harm you, plans to give you hope and a future."

**Jeremiah 29:11**

God is our refuge and strength,
an ever-present help in trouble.

**Psalm 46:1**

So we can say with confidence,

"The Lord is my helper,
so I will have no fear.
What can mere people do to me?"

**Hebrews 13:6 NLT**

Because of the Lord's great love we are not consumed,
for his compassions never fail.

**Lamentations 3:22**

You keep track of all my sorrows.
You have collected all my tears in your bottle.
You have recorded each one in your book.

**Psalm 56:8 NLT**

I press on to reach the end of the race and receive the heavenly prize for which God, through Christ Jesus, is calling us.

**Philippians 3:14 NLT**

But as for you, be strong and do not give up, for your work will be rewarded.

**2 Chronicles 15:7**

Remain in Me, and I [will remain] in you. Just as no branch can bear fruit by itself without remaining in the vine, neither can you [bear fruit, producing evidence of your faith] unless you remain in Me.

**John 15:4 AMP**

But the fruit of the Spirit is love, joy, peace, patience, kindness, goodness, faithfulness, gentleness, self-control; against such things there is no law.

**Galatians 5:22–23 ESV**

Finally, be strong in the Lord and in the strength of his might. Put on the whole armor of God, that you may be able to stand against the schemes of the devil. For we do not wrestle against flesh and blood, but against the rulers, against the authorities, against the cosmic powers over this present darkness, against the spiritual forces of evil in the heavenly places. Therefore take up the whole armor of God, that you may be able to withstand in the evil day, and having done all, to stand firm. Stand therefore, having fastened on the belt of truth, and having put on the breastplate of righteousness, and, as shoes for your feet, having put on the readiness given by the gospel of peace. In all circumstances take up the shield of faith, with which you can extinguish all the flaming darts of the evil one; and take the helmet of salvation, and the sword of the Spirit, which is the word of God.

**Ephesians 6:10–17 ESV**

Every word of God proves true;
he is a shield to those who take refuge in him.

**Proverbs 30:5 ESV**

She is clothed with strength and dignity,
and she laughs without fear of the future.

**Proverbs 31:25 NLT**

Therefore do not worry about tomorrow, for tomorrow will worry about itself. Each day has enough trouble of its own.

**Matthew 6:34**

But for me it is good to be near God;
I have made the Lord God my refuge,
that I may tell of all your works.

**Psalm 73:28 ESV**

Come close to God [with a contrite heart] and He will come close to you. Wash your hands, you sinners; and purify your [unfaithful] hearts, you double-minded [people].

**James 4:8 AMP**

For he himself is our peace, who has made the two groups one and has destroyed the barrier, the dividing wall of hostility, by setting aside in his flesh the law with its commands and regulations. His purpose was to create in himself one new humanity out of the two, thus making peace, and in one body to reconcile both of them to God through the cross, by which he put to death their hostility.

**Ephesians 2:14–16**

I am the vine; you are the branches. If you remain in me and I in you, you will bear much fruit; apart from me you can do nothing.

**John 15:5**

Great peace have those who love your law,
and nothing can make them stumble.

**Psalm 119:165**

For God has not given us a spirit of fear, but of power and of love and of a sound mind.

**2 Timothy 1:7 NKJV**

For God gave us a spirit not of fear but of power and love and self-control.

**2 Timothy 1:7 ESV**

My prayer is not that you take them out of the world but that you protect them from the evil one. They are not of the world, even as I am not of it. Sanctify them by the truth; your word is truth.

**John 17:15–17**

Why, my soul, are you downcast?
  Why so disturbed within me?
Put your hope in God,
  for I will yet praise him,
  my Savior and my God.

**Psalm 43:5**

But those who hope in the Lord
  will renew their strength.
They will soar on wings like eagles;
  they will run and not grow weary,
  they will walk and not be faint.

**Isaiah 40:31**

I have told you these things, so that in me you may have peace. In this world you will have trouble. But take heart! I have overcome the world.

**John 16:33**

Be strong and take heart,
  all you who hope in the Lord.

**Psalm 31:24**

Consider it pure joy, my brothers and sisters, whenever you face trials of many kinds, because you know that the testing of your faith produces perseverance. Let perseverance finish its work so that you may be mature and complete, not lacking anything.

**James 1:2–4**

By his divine power, God has given us everything we need for living a godly life. We have received all of this by coming to know him, the one who called us to himself by means of his marvelous glory and excellence.

**2 Peter 1:3 NLT**

Seek the Kingdom of God above all else, and live righteously, and he will give you everything you need.

**Matthew 6:33 NLT**

For we are his workmanship, created in Christ Jesus for good works, which God prepared beforehand, that we should walk in them.

**Ephesians 2:10 ESV**

"Before I formed you in the womb I knew you,
before you were born I set you apart;
I appointed you as a prophet to the nations."

"Alas, Sovereign Lord," I said, "I do not know how to speak; I am too young."

But the Lord said to me, "Do not say, 'I am too young.' You must go to everyone I send you to and say whatever I command you. Do not be afraid of them, for I am with you and will rescue you," declares the Lord.

**Jeremiah 1:5–8**

For the Lord is good and his love endures forever;
his faithfulness continues through all generations.

**Psalm 100:5**

If we are faithless,
he remains faithful,
for he cannot disown himself.

**2 Timothy 2:13**

This is the confidence we have in approaching God: that if we ask anything according to his will, he hears us.

**1 John 5:14**

This, then, is how you should pray:

"'Our Father in heaven,
hallowed be your name,
your kingdom come,
your will be done,
  on earth as it is in heaven.
Give us today our daily bread.
And forgive us our debts,
  as we also have forgiven our debtors.
And lead us not into temptation,
  but deliver us from the evil one.'"

**Matthew 6:9–13**

My dear children, I write this to you so that you will not sin. But if anybody does sin, we have an advocate with the Father—Jesus Christ, the Righteous One. He is the atoning sacrifice for our sins, and not only for ours but also for the sins of the whole world.

**1 John 2:1–2**

But very truly I tell you, it is for your good that I am going away. Unless I go away, the Advocate will not come to you; but if I go, I will send him to you.

**John 16:7**

In the same way, the Spirit helps us in our weakness. We do not know what we ought to pray for, but the Spirit himself intercedes for us through wordless groans.

**Romans 8:26**

What, then, shall we say in response to these things? If God is for us, who can be against us?

**Romans 8:31**

The LORD is my rock, my fortress, and my savior;
my God is my rock, in whom I find protection.
He is my shield, the power that saves me,
and my place of safety.
He is my refuge, my savior,
the one who saves me from violence.
I called on the LORD, who is worthy of praise,
and he saved me from my enemies.

**2 Samuel 22:2–4 NLT**

God is faithful [He is reliable, trustworthy and ever true to His promise—He can be depended on], and through Him you were called into fellowship with His Son, Jesus Christ our Lord.

**1 Corinthians 1:9 AMP**

Listen to me, O family of Jacob,
Israel my chosen one!
I alone am God,
the First and the Last.
It was my hand that laid the foundations of the earth,
my right hand that spread out the heavens above.
When I call out the stars,
they all appear in order.

**Isaiah 48:12–13 NLT**

If the world hates you, keep in mind that it hated me first. If you belonged to the world, it would love you as its own. As it is, you do not belong to the world, but I have chosen you out of the world. That is why the world hates you.

**John 15:18–19**

Fear of man will prove to be a snare,
 but whoever trusts in the Lord is kept safe.

**Proverbs 29:25**

I will praise the Lord at all times.
 I will constantly speak his praises.
I will boast only in the Lord;
 let all who are helpless take heart.
Come, let us tell of the Lord's greatness;
 let us exalt his name together.

**Psalm 34:1–3 NLT**

Through him then let us continually offer up a sacrifice of praise to God, that is, the fruit of lips that acknowledge his name.

**Hebrews 13:15 ESV**

Consider how the wild flowers grow. They do not labor or spin. Yet I tell you, not even Solomon in all his splendor was dressed like one of these. If that is how God clothes the grass of the field, which is here today, and tomorrow is thrown into the fire, how much more will he clothe you—you of little faith! And do not set your heart on what you will eat or drink; do not worry about it. For the pagan world runs after all such things, and your Father knows that you need them.

**Luke 12:27–30**

Why, you do not even know what will happen tomorrow. What is your life? You are a mist that appears for a little while and then vanishes.

Instead, you ought to say, "If it is the Lord's will, we will live and do this or that."

**James 4:14–15**

No longer do I call you servants, for the servant does not know what his master is doing; but I have called you friends, for all that I have heard from my Father I have made known to you.

**John 15:15 ESV**

A man of many companions may come to ruin,
but there is a friend who sticks closer than a brother.

**Proverbs 18:24 ESV**

Do not conform to the pattern of this world, but be transformed by the renewing of your mind. Then you will be able to test and approve what God's will is—his good, pleasing and perfect will.

**Romans 12:2**

For God has not given us a spirit of fear, but of power and of love and of a sound mind.

**2 Timothy 1:7 NKJV**

Therefore, with minds that are alert and fully sober, set your hope on the grace to be brought to you when Jesus Christ is revealed at his coming.

**1 Peter 1:13**

Therefore, there is now no condemnation for those who are in Christ Jesus, because through Christ Jesus the law of the Spirit who gives life has set you free from the law of sin and death.

**Romans 8:1–2**

For I am convinced that neither death nor life, neither angels nor demons, neither the present nor the future, nor any powers, neither height nor depth, nor anything else in all creation, will be able to separate us from the love of God that is in Christ Jesus our Lord.

**Romans 8:38–39**

There is no fear in love, but perfect love casts out fear. For fear has to do with punishment, and whoever fears has not been perfected in love.

**1 John 4:18 ESV**

This is the day the Lord has made.
We will rejoice and be glad in it.

**Psalm 118:24 NLT**

For no matter how many promises God has made, they are "Yes" in Christ. And so through him the "Amen" is spoken by us to the glory of God.

**2 Corinthians 1:20**

Rejoice always, pray continually, give thanks in all circumstances; for this is God's will for you in Christ Jesus.

**1 Thessalonians 5:16–18**

The Lord will fight for you; you need only to be still.

**Exodus 14:14**

Be still, and know that I am God;
I will be exalted among the nations,
I will be exalted in the earth.

**Psalm 46:10**

Be still before the Lord
and wait patiently for him;

do not fret when people succeed in their ways,
when they carry out their wicked schemes.

**Psalm 37:7**

The Lord will fulfill his purpose for me;
your steadfast love, O Lord, endures forever.
Do not forsake the work of your hands.

**Psalm 138:8 ESV**

For God saved us and called us to live a holy life. He did this, not because we deserved it, but because that was his plan from before the beginning of time—to show us his grace through Christ Jesus.

**2 Timothy 1:9 NLT**

God's way is perfect.
All the Lord's promises prove true.
He is a shield for all who look to him for protection.

**2 Samuel 22:31 NLT**

Jesus replied, "You do not realize now what I am doing, but later you will understand."

**John 13:7**

And I am certain that God, who began the good work within you, will continue his work until it is finally finished on the day when Christ Jesus returns.

**Philippians 1:6 NLT**

Fixing our eyes on Jesus, the pioneer and perfecter of faith. For the joy set before him he endured the cross, scorning its shame, and sat down at the right hand of the throne of God.

**Hebrews 12:2**

Surely the righteous will never be shaken;
 they will be remembered forever.
They will have no fear of bad news;
 their hearts are steadfast, trusting in the Lord.
Their hearts are secure, they will have no fear;
 in the end they will look in triumph on their foes.

**Psalm 112:6–8**

To all who mourn in Israel,
 he will give a crown of beauty for ashes,
a joyous blessing instead of mourning,
 festive praise instead of despair.
In their righteousness, they will be like great oaks
 that the Lord has planted for his own glory.

**Isaiah 61:3 NLT**

And those who belong to Christ Jesus have crucified the flesh with its passions and desires. If we live by the Spirit, let us also keep in step with the Spirit.

**Galatians 5:24–25 ESV**

Many are the plans in a person's heart,
 but it is the Lord's purpose that prevails.

**Proverbs 19:21**

The Lord will guide you always;
 he will satisfy your needs in a sun-scorched land
 and will strengthen your frame.
You will be like a well-watered garden,
 like a spring whose waters never fail.

**Isaiah 58:11**

Trust in *and* rely confidently on the Lord with all your heart
And do not rely on your own insight *or* understanding.

In all your ways know *and* acknowledge *and* recognize Him,
And He will make your paths straight *and* smooth
[removing obstacles that block your way]."

**Proverbs 3:5–6 AMP**

I pray that God, the source of hope, will fill you completely with joy and peace because you trust in him. Then you will overflow with confident hope through the power of the Holy Spirit.

**Romans 15:13 NLT**

Let us hold fast the confession of our hope without wavering, for he who promised is faithful.

**Hebrews 10:23 ESV**

My sheep listen to my voice; I know them, and they follow me.

**John 10:27**

## Additional Scriptures

I've included a few extra Scriptures to encourage your heart and help you replace fear, anxiety, and worry with the truth of God's Word. Remember that His Word is your greatest weapon.

Whoever dwells in the shelter of the Most High
will rest in the shadow of the Almighty.
I will say of the Lord, "He is my refuge and my fortress,
my God, in whom I trust."

Surely he will save you
from the fowler's snare
and from the deadly pestilence.

He will cover you with his feathers,
and under his wings you will find refuge;
his faithfulness will be your shield and rampart.
You will not fear the terror of night,
nor the arrow that flies by day,
nor the pestilence that stalks in the darkness,
nor the plague that destroys at midday.
A thousand may fall at your side,
ten thousand at your right hand,
but it will not come near you.
You will only observe with your eyes
and see the punishment of the wicked.

If you say, "The Lord is my refuge,"
and you make the Most High your dwelling,
no harm will overtake you,
no disaster will come near your tent.
For he will command his angels concerning you
to guard you in all your ways;
they will lift you up in their hands,
so that you will not strike your foot against a stone.
You will tread on the lion and the cobra;
you will trample the great lion and the serpent.

"Because he loves me," says the Lord, "I will rescue him;
I will protect him, for he acknowledges my name.
He will call on me, and I will answer him;
I will be with him in trouble,
I will deliver him and honor him.
With long life I will satisfy him
and show him my salvation."

**Psalm 91**

Therefore I tell you, do not worry about your life, what you will eat or drink; or about your body, what you will wear. Is not life more than food, and the body more than clothes? Look at the birds of the air; they do not sow or reap or store away in barns, and yet your heavenly Father feeds them. Are you not much more valuable than they? Can any one of you by worrying add a single hour to your life?

**Matthew 6:25–27**

I sought the Lord, and he answered me;
he delivered me from all my fears.

**Psalm 34:4**

Say to those with fearful hearts,
"Be strong, and do not fear,
for your God is coming to destroy your enemies.
He is coming to save you."

**Isaiah 35:4 NLT**

Now the Lord is the Spirit, and where the Spirit of the Lord is, there is freedom.

**2 Corinthians 3:17**

But when I am afraid,
I will put my trust in you.
I praise God for what he has promised.
I trust in God, so why should I be afraid?
What can mere mortals do to me?

**Psalm 56:3–4 NLT**

But he said to me, "My grace is sufficient for you, for my power is made perfect in weakness." Therefore I will boast all the more gladly about my weaknesses, so that Christ's power may rest on me.

**2 Corinthians 12:9**

Praise be to the Lord, to God our Savior,
who daily bears our burdens.

**Psalm 68:19**

For you did not receive the spirit of slavery to fall back into fear, but you have received the Spirit of adoption as sons, by whom we cry, "Abba! Father!"

**Romans 8:15 ESV**

When my anxious thoughts multiply within me,
Your comforts delight me.

**Psalm 94:19 AMP**

The Lord God is my strength [my source of courage, my
invincible army];
He has made my feet [steady and sure] like hinds' feet
And makes me walk [forward with spiritual confidence] on
my high places [of challenge and responsibility].

**Habakkuk 3:19 AMP**

But the Lord is faithful, and he will strengthen you and protect you from the evil one.

**2 Thessalonians 3:3**

Anxiety in a man's heart weighs him down,
but a good word makes him glad.

**Proverbs 12:25 ESV**

I know what it is to be in need, and I know what it is to have plenty. I have learned the secret of being content in any and every situation, whether well fed or hungry, whether living in plenty or in want. I can do all this through him who gives me strength.

**Philippians 4:12–13**

Because God's children are human beings—made of flesh and blood—the Son also became flesh and blood. For only as a human being could he die, and only by dying could he break the power of the devil, who had the power of death. Only in this way could he set free all who have lived their lives as slaves to the fear of dying.

**Hebrews 2:14–15 NLT**

Even though I walk through the valley of the shadow of death,
  I will fear no evil,
for you are with me;
  your rod and your staff,
  they comfort me.

**Psalm 23:4 ESV**

Be on your guard; stand firm in the faith; be courageous; be strong.

**1 Corinthians 16:13**

Fear not, little flock, for it is your Father's good pleasure to give you the kingdom.

**Luke 12:32 ESV**

When you lie down, you will not be afraid;
  when you lie down, your sleep will be sweet.

**Proverbs 3:24**

In him our hearts rejoice,
  for we trust in his holy name.

**Psalm 33:21**

Now may the God of peace, who through the blood of the eternal covenant brought back from the dead our Lord Jesus, that great Shepherd of the sheep, equip you with everything good for doing his will, and may he work in us what is pleasing to him, through Jesus Christ, to whom be glory for ever and ever. Amen.

**Hebrews 13:20–21**

From the ends of the earth I call to you,
I call as my heart grows faint;
lead me to the rock that is higher than I.

**Psalm 61:2**

For the Lord your God is living among you.
He is a mighty savior.
He will take delight in you with gladness.
With his love, he will calm all your fears.
He will rejoice over you with joyful songs.

**Zephaniah 3:17 NLT**

I lift up my eyes to the mountains—
where does my help come from?
My help comes from the Lord,
the Maker of heaven and earth.

**Psalm 121:1–2**

But the Lord is faithful, and he will strengthen you and protect you from the evil one.

**2 Thessalonians 3:3**

You, dear children, are from God and have overcome them, because the one who is in you is greater than the one who is in the world.

**1 John 4:4**

Therefore, there is now no condemnation for those who are in Christ Jesus, because through Christ Jesus the law of the Spirit who gives life has set you free from the law of sin and death.

**Romans 8:1–2**

The name of the Lord is a strong tower;
the righteous man runs into it and is safe.

**Proverbs 18:10 ESV**

Trust in him at all times, you people;
pour out your hearts to him,
for God is our refuge.

**Psalm 62:8**

For no word from God will ever fail.

**Luke 1:37**

**MADDIE JOY FISCHER** is a twenty-six-year-old writer, speaker, and worship leader in St. Louis, Missouri. She is a wife, the oldest of five siblings, and a born-and-raised pastor's kid. She is also an ambassador (writer) for the LO sister app by Sadie Robertson's ministry, Live Original. Maddie's passion is to point people to Jesus through living a life of surrender. For ten years, she has shared this passion on her social media platforms with a desire to see people grow in knowledge of God's Word, boldness to proclaim it, and love for the One who it's all about. She continues to take every opportunity she is given to live out the calling God has prepared for her life as He has continued to grow her ministry every step of the way.

**CONNECT WITH MADDIE**

**MaddieeJoy.com**

 @MaddieFischer  @Maddiee_Joy

# Rest + Rely

Books by Maddie Joy Fischer

*Trust + Follow*
*Rest + Rely*